Learning
My Living

Gaye Manwaring

LEARNING MY LIVING

Reflections on Teaching in Higher Education for Over Fifty Years

Dr Gaye Manwaring MBE

BSc; Dip Anim Gen; PhD; TQ;
FHEA; FRSA

Learning My Living: Reflections on Teaching in Higher Education for Over Fifty Years by Gaye Manwaring.

First edition published in Great Britain in 2022 by Extremis Publishing Ltd., Suite 218, Castle House, 1 Baker Street, Stirling, FK8 1AL, United Kingdom. *www.extremispublishing.com*

Extremis Publishing is a Private Limited Company registered in Scotland (SC509983) whose Registered Office is Suite 218, Castle House, 1 Baker Street, Stirling, FK8 1AL, United Kingdom.

A CIP catalogue record for this book is available from the British Library.

ISBN: 978-1-7398543-1-7

Typeset in Goudy Bookletter 1911, designed by The League of Moveable Type.
Printed and bound in Great Britain by IngramSpark, Chapter House, Pitfield, Kiln Farm, Milton Keynes, MK11 3LW, United Kingdom.

This book is dedicated to my wonderful husband,

Andy Wilson

He has supported and encouraged me throughout my career and into retirement.

Contents

Foreword

"Education is not preparation for life;
education is life itself."
John Dewey (1897)

I have known Gaye Manwaring for over forty years. I have been her student, her colleague, her co-author, her team-teaching buddy, her driver and a member of her 'fine dining' circle. Most of all she has been a life-long critical friend.

Gaye has an amazing life story to tell, and this memoir focuses only on one tiny aspect of her incredible life: her role as an educator. No ordinary educator as you will see. This collection of personal memories relates to specific aspects in her life as a teacher in higher education and provides insights, perspectives, and points for reflection as she describes her relationship to and feelings about education, educational processes, and her life as a facilitator of learning.

Gaye has worked across the world, and I had the opportunity to work alongside her in far-flung places from Belfast to Eritrea. Her ability to connect, engage and inspire, and in so doing transform individual learners' lives, is powerful to observe. But the work does not stop when the lesson ends. Gaye continues to support many of her past students to this day. Mentoring and life-long support are not optional extras. They come with the package.

Gaye has dedicated her life to education and her students, and she constantly and untiringly empowers them to succeed in whatever walk of life they inhabit. Few educators have taught professionals from across the occupational spectrum and from such a diverse range of countries. Her ability to adapt and tailor-make the learning experience is exceptional.

It is an honour to be invited to write this foreword for such an outstanding educator.

William Ian Ball
Professor of Education (retired)
The University of Dundee

Places and Dates

Institution	Date
Garlinge Infant School, Margate, Kent	September 1950
Garlinge Primary School, Margate, Kent	September 1952
Clarendon House Grammar School, Ramsgate, Kent	September 1955
Wallingford Grammar School, Wallingford, Berkshire	November 1955
Didcot Girls' Grammar School, Didcot, Berkshire	September 1957
The University of Exeter, Exeter, Devon	October 1963
The University of Edinburgh, Edinburgh	October 1966
The University of Glasgow, Glasgow	April 1969
Dundee College of Education, Dundee	April 1975
Northern College (Dundee Campus), Dundee	July 1987
The University of Dundee (Gardyne Campus), Dundee	December 2001
The University of Dundee (City Campus), Dundee	July 2006
Retirement	May 2020

Country	Dates	Purpose
Poland	1974	Conference
USA	1974	Conference. Study tour. Research
Canada	1974	Study tour. Research
Malaysia	1978, 1979	Staff development*
Thailand	1978	Staff development*
Australia	1979	Staff development*. Study tour. Research
Netherlands	1980	Teaching (DipEdTech). Consultancy
Northern Ireland	1992, 1993	Staff development (BAPD)*
Eire	2002	Conference
Eritrea	2005	Teaching (BAPD). Consultancy
Croatia	2007	Staff development*. Consultancy

*Staff development refers to me running workshops and individual support for academic staff in the institutions I visited. It was not staff development for me but I did learn a great deal from the experiences.

DipEdTech = Postgraduate Diploma in Educational Technology

BAPD = BA in Professional Development

I have also added a short curriculum vitae at the end of this book.

LEARNING MY LIVING

Gaye Manwaring

Introduction

ALWAYS write the introduction last. Good advice. I had written over half of the book before I had worked out the best way to organise it. I never intended to write this book. The whole idea seemed too self-indulgent, and I did not think anyone would be that interested in me or my career. When I retired as a senior lecturer after working for half a century in higher education I wrote to my colleagues to thank them for their very generous gifts, and I shared a few stories from my academic life. Several people enjoyed the anecdotes and asked for more. A few weeks later I was talking to a new friend who asked me about some of the countries I had visited in my career, and she was fascinated by my insights. Then the Covid-19 pandemic caused lockdown, so I looked for something to occupy my time and my mind and I started to write this chronicle.

I was not sure of the best way to structure it. Obviously there was the chronology, but I also noticed certain themes that kept cropping up. Some of these clustered naturally within the time frame, while others seemed to fit better as a consolidation at the end. Normally when I communicate I know my audience and I can interact with them, tailoring my words to their interests. It is much harder writing in a vacuum and hoping that my unknown public will want to read it. I was unsure of the balance between providing information about education and giving a personal perspective. I had to stop myself from writing an academic thesis. I tried to avoid the passive tense and to ignore the urge to cite references to literature.

As I wrote I remembered things, people and places I had forgotten, but often I did recall some of the emotions and the learning which I carried forward. I referred to old photographs and reports and articles written at the time, and I have included a few extracts. Some topics occupied large chunks of my life but I found I had very little of interest to say about them. How I wish I had kept some of the items I threw out in a decluttering binge. How I wish I knew where my photos of America, Poland and Australia went!

Now I can notice patterns in my life. I did not seek opportunities, but I took them when they were offered. I was not ambitious in the traditional sense but I wanted a career that was challenging and interesting for me, and meaningful and helpful to others. One of the first tasks we give to new university lecturers is to ask them to consider the qualities of a good teacher in higher education and to begin to formulate their own personal philosophy of teaching and learning. They write something between a creed and a manifesto, and consider the challenges that sometimes make it hard to enact it. Pressures from formal regulations and informal ethos tensions mean that compromise may sometimes be needed. I can now see some of the influences that shaped my own philosophy of teaching and learning, and which affected the way I behave.

I did not want to do research, and I feel that too much prestige is attached to research activities compared to quality teaching. Research in medicine and engineering has a clear purpose, but research in social sciences is less obvious in its value. There is so much pressure on academics to publish that some publish too soon, or rehash their material for different journals. Supervisors add their name to the work done by their students, so their own tally increases. My view is unpopular but some staff do spend a lot of time focusing on research and feel that teaching is a necessary evil. Some teaching staff feel that what they do is seen as less important than research, and they think that they are less valued as people. Such inequalities and discriminatory attitudes seem to be prevalent in education as in other walks of life.

I loved the university environment, and academia suited me. I have taken lots of courses in my lifetime, but much of my "real learning" occurred in other ways that were often informal, unplanned and unexpected. My career in higher education involved teaching many students on different courses. I worked on a wide range of development projects and visited ten countries.

I travelled to many European countries with family and friends and had some wonderful experiences: a gondola trip in Venice, the Tivoli Gardens in Copenhagen, Murano glass, hydrangea hedges in the Azores, the Port Wine Institute in Lisbon. But these are all standard tourist attractions. When I visited places as part of my academic work I saw a different side. I met the locals and saw the country through their eyes, which gave me a more authentic adventure. And all those trips were free of charge to me.

Although the main focus of this book is my role in delivering higher education, I felt I should start earlier in my life so I began with my childhood, schooldays and student life. I was born just after the end of the Second World War and lived with my parents in Margate, Kent until I was ten and we moved to Berkshire. I did my first degree at the University of Exeter, followed by a doctorate at the University of Edinburgh. I was employed as a research fellow at the University of Glasgow for six years before moving to Dundee College of Education as a senior lecturer. The college was involved in mergers that led to being part of the University of Dundee, where I stayed until I retired at the age of seventy-five as required by the pension provider. Thinking about my career, remembering the varied experiences and reliving the emotions has been cathartic and has given me a sense of closure.

I have always been an avid learner, curious and keen to apply new ideas. I like to make connections between things and to find ways to encourage others to learn. I hope teachers of any kind will find the educational ideas and activities useful and adaptable. I hope my readers will find the book interesting and entertaining, and will think about their own educational experiences.

I am an academic, and this is my story.

Part 1: Learning

Chapter One

Childhood

Parent Power

I was an only child, and I had a good relationship with my parents. They taught me to read and write and other skills such as cooking, sewing and driving, and gave me a love of books and of nature. They were always supportive but never pushy. They also gave me values, setting my moral compass, although this was unintentional and probably unconscious. They simply acted as role models. They respected personal property; they would never open each other's mail; my Dad would not open my Mum's handbag; she would not look in his wallet. They encouraged me to explain my reasons for doing things. When I was four I would eat bread and jam upside down. Instead of asking me to stop, they asked me why. I explained that it meant that I could taste the sweet jam more immediately, so it made sense, even if it was sometimes messy. They were careful with money. Every Friday night, after payday, they would get out the green leather bag that held a dozen tins and jars labelled 'housekeeping', 'electricity', 'rates', 'clothes', 'holidays', 'spare', etc. – and, intriguingly, 'real spare'. Cash was allocated to each pot in turn. This taught me the value of money and the importance of budgeting and planning.

Me, aged thirteen, with Mum and Dad.

The Festival of Britain in the summer of 1951 is a key memory. My parents and I stayed with relatives in Middlesex and travelled up to London each day. I was entranced by the Underground, though I misread some of the station names. Black Friars became "Black Fairies", and Charing Cross was "Charging Cross". I am not dyslexic, but I related what I read to concepts I already knew. The exhibition was full of people in strange costumes, exotic music and lots of exciting things. I had been in a lift in a department store at home, but a moving staircase from America was new and intriguing.

We were not gamblers, but my Uncle Harry always did the football pools and had a flutter on the horses. One day when I was about seven he asked me if I wanted him to place a bet for me, so I chose a horse and asked him to put on sixpence each way. It was called Downstream and it was a real outsider, but it won at 40/1. My Uncle gave me my guinea for my winnings and I was delighted. At least ten years later he told me that he had not wanted me to waste my money, so had not actually put my bet on. He had paid me out of his own pocket when the outsider romped home. What a kind and honest gesture.

Money was tight for many people and our neighbours took in paying guests for bed and breakfast. Margate was, after all, a seaside resort. One time, they were busy and asked if we could have their regular visitors instead. Mum and Dad agreed, mostly to help out the neighbours. A few months later, they wanted to visit us again instead of the neighbours; apparently our house was quieter and the breakfast was much better: bacon and egg rather than cornflakes. My parents said no, as they did not want to risk upsetting the neighbours – an important lesson in priorities and values.

Another childhood memory is about fish. My Dad asked why we were eating sprats when my Mum had gone to the fishmonger to buy the more expensive plaice that he liked. She explained that while waiting in the queue the woman behind had complained about the price of food and how she was struggling. My Mum felt it would be insensitive to buy such a luxury as plaice so she asked for a much cheaper catch. Her kindness to spare a stranger's feelings was typical – and we all enjoyed the tasty sprats.

The worst crime was lying, and I thought this was odd. Surely violence or stealing were worse? But I eventually realised how important trust was and how key to legal processes. My parents were lifelong Labour voters, and I followed their lead. When I was only about seven I responded to a neighbour who was complaining about price rises by saying "It's those flipping Tories!" Much later when I was old enough to think about social justice I chose to support Labour too.

My Dad took me on a three-day camping trip when I was eight. He fixed a child seat on his push bike and we had one tiny tent. For me it was all fun and excitement, but there was a lot of learning, too, about respect for private property and for nature. We asked permission to camp in the woods belonging to a farmer, and his wife gave us some eggs. I helped to pitch the tent, learned how to make a campfire and deal with it properly when we left.

My parents treated me with trust and respect so that I felt I was a part of the family, not just a junior member. I did not feel like a child. When I was twelve we moved into our own bungalow and money was tight. I volunteered to give up half of my pocket money. The financial impact would have been minimal, but it made me feel I was making a contribution.

Infant School

I started at Garlinge Infants School in Margate a month before my fifth birthday in 1950, and I could already read and write. At a pre-entry meeting at my infant school I was asked to thread some coloured beads onto a string after the teacher had demonstrated the sequence. I do not know if it was testing manual dexterity, colour vision or comprehension. I do know I did it correctly and speedily, and thought that it was a stupid task and wondered how this establishment would teach me anything if that was the level of instruction.

On my way out, accompanied by my mother, I ran along the corridor. An elderly teacher yelled at me that if I ran I would trip and bang my head on one of the metal radiators and bleed to death. It did not stop me running in the future, but I was scared of radiators and of her. I do remember the incident, but I do not feel there was any sense of care and protection – just of control and adherence to the rules. Was it really a good idea to make my first memory of school such a negative one? Is fear ever a good motivator? The archetypical drill sergeant shouting at the new army recruits comes to mind, but I am not sure if it has a place in education. I have seen students almost frozen in fear that a tutor would ask them to speak. This was not necessarily a lack of knowledge but a crisis of confidence, and a worry about looking foolish in front of peers. Creating a positive environment and encouraging students to discuss ideas in pairs before sharing them can alleviate such fears.

Thinking back now, I can visualise my infant classroom. The ceilings were very high and the windows were placed above our eye level, so we received the daylight but could not see the outside world or get distracted by it. Each afternoon we had half an hour of play when the teacher handed out toys. I soon realised that some toys were good quality and others were pathetic, old and boring. I also noticed that the same pupils always got the best toys regardless of how well we had behaved or performed. Even at my tender age I felt the unfairness of this. I was polite and bright but I never got a good toy, and I did not know what to do to improve my chances.

I vividly remember one assembly when a girl who was frequently in trouble was punished publicly. The headmistress led her onto the stage, lifted her skirt, pulled down her knickers and smacked her bare bottom. If this was meant as a deterrent to the rest of us, it failed. We were shocked but we did not know what her crime had been, so we could not make the connection between deed and consequence. This public humiliation was presumably intended as a warning to stop the rest of us behaving badly, but we did not know the context. Learning often depends on making the correct links between a new experience and existing knowledge. The teacher can suggest the relationships or the learner can make their own connections, but they are needed as the essential scaffolding of learning and understanding.

Primary School

A couple of years later I moved to Garlinge Primary School next door. It was rather cold and bleak, but there were large areas of grass where we would play at breaktime. One of our favourite haunts was the air raid shelter: a reminder of the war. It was locked and out of bounds, but the steps down to its entrance were always inviting and a bit scary.

The morning assembly was quite boring, but I enjoyed the singing. We sat cross-legged on the floor of the hall and the headmaster, who was a bully, walked around casually kicking boys (only boys) for no apparent reason. We accepted this as normal behaviour, and were not surprised that the kicks seemed to be random. Somehow it would have been more understandable if he had kicked out in anger in response to bad behaviour. I realised early on that the girls were usually safe.

I did well at school and still remember one class written

Class with Mr Pyne. I am second left in the front row.

test. We were asked whether "funeral" music would be happy or sad. I knew the word but I had never seen it written down, but I applied some logic. The first part of the word was "fun" so I answered that the music would be happy. I was quite upset that my answer was marked wrong and I was not given any credit. After all, in maths the working out counted even if the final answer was wrong. I felt sympathy when something similar happened to a friend. We were asked the words for the animal and plant life of a region. I knew the correct answer was "flora and fauna", but my friend was stumped. She thought she knew half the answer, so she gave the answer as "vegetation and animation". I felt confused by the actions of another pupil in a geography class. We had to draw a circle to represent the world and add in a diameter linked to the magnetic north. This was meant to be on a slight tilt, not a vertical line. As the teacher explained this I saw two pupils get out their rubbers. One rubbed out the line and added the correct one. Another, to my amazement, rubbed out the circle so she could tilt it.

Our teacher for sewing and knitting was a small, grumpy, grey lady, and we nicknamed her "Miss Sandypants". One day I approached her desk for help with my knitting which had developed some problems. She was focused on some paperwork and ignored me. After a while, feeling exposed waiting at the front I asked if she could please help me. She rounded on me and slapped my face. It was not hard but I was shocked and mortified and returned to my seat, crying quietly. She looked up and saw my tear-stained face and asked what I was snivelling about. When I said she had hit me, she seemed confused. I think she had hit me automatically and immediately forgot about it, but it was big deal for me and even now I can remember feeling angry and somehow ashamed.

We had several school trips. We went to Dover Castle, where we were locked in a dungeon – but only for a few minutes. I did not enjoy Whipsnade Zoo because, although I love animals, I did not like seeing them looking bored in dingy cages. We visited Margate gas works, where I was amazed to see that coal gas was cleaned using scrubbing brushes. Our trip to Sturry woods was cut short by a heavy storm, but not before we had caught tadpoles in the river. When the Queen came to visit the town we all lined up outside the station and waved union jacks as she passed by. There were no excursions at secondary school apart from biology field trips; perhaps by then the focus was on the formal curriculum.

Every year the school had a gala with games and competitions. One year we all decorated our bikes or tricycles with coloured ribbons. Later that term we dressed up as mediaeval knights and ladies, still for some strange reason on bikes. Another time it was fancy dress and I went as Mr Cube, an advertising avatar for Tate and Lyle sugar. My Dad sent away for some posters and covered a cardboard box, which I wore. The box was really uncomfortable, and I remember having cold legs. I carried a two-pound bag of sugar, which I dropped. Later when I

Gala day at primary school.

saw the photos I was embarrassed that everyone could see my knickers, but I did not realise it at the time. I did not mind not winning, but I was disappointed that the prize-winners were all princesses or fairies. The judges did not appreciate originality. The following year my Dad made me a hat which was a lantern with a switch to turn the bulb on and off. The winners were boring examples of millinery decorated with feathers and flowers. The real problem was that the judges did not make their criteria explicit.

Fancy dress as Mr Cube.

I remember one very unsavoury incident. The girls' toilets were smeared with excrement on several occasions. Within a few days the teachers had identified and suspended the culprit. She was not from my class, and I did not know her well. At the time the focus seemed to be all about punishment, but I wonder now what caused a mild-mannered, quietly spoken nine-year-old girl to behave in such a way. Was she mentally ill, was this a cry for help, or was it (as the teachers suggested) mere naughtiness?

I had been off ill for a couple of days and so had missed the request to bring in some magazine pictures of foreign places to stick into a personal "Journey Book". We had to write a story around the pictures. The pupils began sorting and sticking their coloured pictures into their books and a girl (not a particular friend) gave me a picture of flamenco dancers in Spain. It was such a kind gesture. It was the only resource I had that day so my journey had to start in Spain and that set the route for the next few weeks. This almost seems like a metaphor for many of the turning points in my life initiated by chance. Writing this, seventy years later, is my own journey book of places I actually visited.

The eleven-plus exam was a selection process to determine which type of secondary school you attended: the more academic environment of a grammar school or a secondary modern. On the morning we sat the exam we were released as soon as it was over and allowed to go home, even though it was half an hour before the normal lunch break. I ran home and my Mum was surprised to see me. I teased her by saying I had left because I could not answer any questions. She immediately cuddled me and said it did not matter, although I still believe it did matter. I took and passed my eleven-plus exam when I was only ten and was all set to go to Clarendon House Grammar School, which was my first choice. This was the sister school of Chatham House, which had been attended by my father and by the future prime minister Edward Heath. Both schools were in Ramsgate and it took about twenty-five minutes to get there by bus.

In the summer of 1955 my father got a new job as a librarian at the Medical Research Council's radiobiology lab in Harwell, Berkshire. We moved into a flat in Harwell village, and Berkshire County Council informed my parents that I would attend the village primary school. Unlike Kent, Berkshire schools took the selection exam at the age of eleven to twelve so I was expected to go back to primary school for a year, take the eleven-plus exam (again) and, if successful, go to Wallingford Grammar School. My parents were horrified at this proposed setback to my schooling, but a very sympathetic secretary at Berkshire Education Department had a good idea. She explained that if I started secondary school in Kent and then moved to Berkshire, they would not be able to put me back. So I stayed with my grandparents in Margate for five weeks and started at Clarendon House in Ramsgate, wearing the uniform of Wallingford Grammar. The headmistress there was welcoming and understanding but was concerned that I might feel uncomfortable dressed differently from the other girls, though I was fine because I was with my friends. At half term I joined my parents in Harwell and went to my new school. There I was not only a new late arrival but I did not know anyone, and I felt a bit of an outsider for as long as two years. I was the youngest in the class, and needed a special dispensation to take my "O" Levels at my tender age. Fortunately I passed them all, vindicating the decision.

Secondary School

I was at Wallingford for two years, which was very convenient as we had moved into the town. My Dad had designed a bungalow with many lovely features. The bathroom and toilet had round windows like large portholes. The fireplace in the lounge had a slit window on each side, fitted with yellow glass that gave a golden glow when the sun shone. The roof was covered with green tiles, and the patio had multi-coloured paving slabs.

Wallingford Grammar was a famous old school, established in 1672. The main buildings were grand, but the lower classes were housed in portacabins at the back. They were draughty in winter and sometimes the noise of the wind and rain almost drowned out the teacher's voice. In summer they were hot and airless. I felt shy as the only new person joining a few weeks late, but I soon made friends and got a prize at the end of first year. The first-year classes were 1Q, 1P and 1R, but by second year we had been labelled. The brightest pupils were put in 2A, a mixed class. The less bright boys were in 2B and the girls in 2C. I was so relieved that I was in 2A but my best friend, Janet, was in 2C. Not only were we separated, but one of the teachers told me I should pick different friends from my own class. I wonder if the teachers ever stopped to think about the danger and unfairness of deeming someone "inferior" at such a young age.

The French and Latin teacher waved his arms so that his black gown made him look like a giant bat. He would a call an unfortunate pupil (always a boy) out to the front. He would then ask the class questions and any wrong answers resulted in him hitting the boy at the front with the cane. He seemed to choose unpopular pupils so some of the other boys would give the wrong answer deliberately. By chance, my father had endured the same teacher with the same appalling teaching style at Chatham House.

I do not remember any racial diversity in the school. Indeed, there was very little in the town at that time. Catholic pupils were excused from the morning assembly, which seemed strange since they missed out on any information as well as the hymns and prayers. The music teacher was very opposed to this discrimination. I remember him yelling at the two catholic pupils in my class when we rehearsed for the carol service. He said they were no better than the rest of us and they were required to sing. I noticed that the boy next to me only mouthed the words and did not sing, and I silently applauded this small act of rebellion. Fortunately, schools are much more inclusive now and celebrate a range of religious music.

Wallingford was mixed, but the authorities built a new school in Didcot that became the girls' school while Wallingford became only for boys. This meant that I had a long bus journey again to get to school. We were sad to leave our friends. The headmistress of the new school was a Miss Holloway, so of course the school was nicknamed "Holloway Jail." The summer uniform was a grey and white striped cotton dress which made us look like convicts, although the winter uniform of grey skirt and royal blue blazer was smart. She was a strange, intense lady. If you were ever in trouble she would reel off all the misdemeanours ever perpetrated by anybody in your class. This seemed unfair and bizarre, and while we felt some fear we did not feel respect for her. Our new headmistress was snobbish too, and did not like us to maintain contact with our old school. When we had a school dance we had to invite boys from a posh fee-paying school in Abingdon and not our erstwhile classmates from Wallingford.

Another case of unjustifiable superiority was in relation to the nearby secondary modern school. We tended to regard the school and its pupils as poorer in every way, not just of lower intelligence (whatever that means) but as rude and untrustworthy. There was little suggestion then of late bloomers, or of valuing personal qualities other than the ability to pass exams. This was a case of brainwashing; insidious and probably unintentional, but I am sure it will have had a negative impact on those who perceived themselves as failures. I remember my Dad telling me he had bumped into a school friend's parent soon after I graduated. They exchanged news of their children with my Dad proud of my degree. Val's father said she and her husband had just had their first child, but "anyone can have a baby."

I have seen so many instances of people who did poorly at school, yet blossomed later, often because the motivation to learn became internal rather than external, and because the style of learning was more suited to them. I have also heard from employers who were frustrated with academic high-fliers who had poor soft skills. They might have knowledge but if they were lazy, rude, late and unreliable they did not make good employees. Educational establishments may encourage competition but teamwork, collaboration and interpersonal communication skills may be more useful. Creative approaches may be frowned upon and penalised with poor grades, but without innovation we could not flourish. I think society is now becoming more accepting of individual differences and more appreciative of different skillsets.

Now we are aware of unconscious bias and micro-aggression, and how much harm such attitudes can do. Every day a couple of squirrels visit our garden and play on the bank at the back and we delight in watching their antics. Whenever I mention them to anyone, the first comment is always whether they are red or grey, with the tacit implication that red is best. This is so unfair. The squirrels do not know they are an immigrant species, and what could they do about it anyway?

I felt no great allegiance to Didcot Girls' Grammar School, although some of the teachers were great. I do not remember any school clubs and the only extracurricular activities were related to sports, which did not interest me. If you forgot your PE kit, you had to tidy up the games cupboard. Some saw this as a punishment but I preferred it to freezing on the hockey field or being yelled at on the tennis court. The teacher was always telling me I was in "no man's land" without ever explaining what it meant or how to get out of it. However, we were all excited when Ann Packer jumped 19 feet and 5 inches in the long jump on sports day as this was her entry into national athletics. She later won Olympic gold as a sprinter in 1964.

I am shy and was quite reserved at school. I hated reading aloud in class, but I scored good marks for reciting a poem in a speech competition. It was T. S. Eliot's "The Journey of the Magi," and I was told I rendered it with clarity and passion. It is still one of my favourite poems. I worked hard and was always in the top three in my form, but many school reports remarked "Gaye should speak up more in class." I did not see why this concerned them. I now accept how much lurkers can gain from silent engagement with online courses. But I also now understand that all school pupils should be encouraged to communicate effectively and to develop the confidence to speak in public. I think my teachers would have been surprised to learn about my successful public speaking in my career – much easier when you have an official role and title.

The curriculum in the lower school was broad and included needlework and cookery. We made a needle case, an embroidered gingham apron and a summer skirt. One time we made a fish pie to take home and I left mine on the school bus. I do not think the food was much of a loss, but my Mum missed her Pyrex dish. From fourth year we had to choose a more limited range of subjects, although English, maths, biology and French were compulsory for all. I selected Latin over art, chemistry over cookery, physics over needlework and geography over history.

I remember a powerful lesson in learner responsibility. It was during a biology lesson at the start of fifth year when we would take "O" Level exams. The teacher explained the syllabus for the year and talked about the mix of classwork, practicals and homework. Then she said that it was up to us to work hard and getting a good grade was in our own hands. I was shocked. I had never really thought about it, but I assumed that if I did what the teacher told me I would succeed. Now she seemed to be abdicating her responsibility, but of course she was right. Learners of all ages will progress better if they assume some autonomy over their studies.

We were given an individual interview with a careers adviser in fifth year so we could choose our "A" Level subjects. But the only options she suggested to me (and to my classmates) were nursing or teaching. Neither vocation was appealing, although I did not have any particular careers in mind. Looking back, many of my life choices seem to have been unplanned but fairly lucky.

On 3rd February 1959 the pop star Buddy Holly was killed in a plane crash. Everyone in the class was devastated, as we were great fans. We decided to hold a two-minute silence at 11 o'clock. Unfortunately at the agreed time we were in a chemistry lesson, and the poor teacher must have wondered what was wrong with her usually well-behaved pupils as we all refused to answer her questions. She was beginning to lose her patience when the time was up and we returned to our normal compliant selves.

I loved English and Latin, but decided that it would be easier to learn the arts by myself and that I would benefit more by being taught the sciences. I was really upset when my Latin teacher committed suicide. She was a lovely young, vibrant person; it seemed such a sad waste. At "A" Level we had two excellent biology teachers. Mrs Watson was married to a teacher from another school who had written books on mosses and liverworts. She invited us to her home to meet him and have an informal tutorial.

Mrs Pratt took us on a course to a field studies centre on the banks of Windemere in the Lake

At the Lake District.

District. We explored the flora and fauna of the lake and the mountains. The centre offered sixpence each for any frogs or toads that we collected. Most of us managed to find one or two, but a couple of my classmates turned up with five amphibians. They later admitted that they had found the tank in the basement that held the creatures. They had liberated a few and returned them for extra cash.

Another field trip was a few days at Juniper Hall Field Studies Centre. It was a beautiful location in the Surrey countryside, and the course was interesting. One of the speakers was Professor Dowdeswell, who would become an important person in my professional life seven years later. Another significant person was David from a school in Devon. We became firm platonic friends and spent many holidays together visiting museums and art galleries in London and exploring the Scottish Highlands by hitchhiking and youth hostelling.

I applied to do some doorstep interviews with Gallup Poll and was asked to do a few sample surveys. After enquiring about various products I had to ask what social class the

At Juniper Hall with David.

person belonged to. One lady said she was lower class because they did not have much money. I tried to explain that it was not all about money, but she replied that they were definitely lower social class because they did not go out much and were not very sociable. So I ticked the box for lower class, but I reflected on how accurate the classification of participants could be if they and the interviewers did not agree on the definitions. Years later I thought about the whole issue of informed consent when interviewees did not understand enough to be able to give permission.

I took a holiday job as a waitress in a riverside restaurant. I was paid one shilling and sixpence per hour, which went up to half a crown (two shillings and sixpence) after my trial week. One evening someone ordered a boiled egg, which was not on the menu. The owner agreed to the request but said that the charge would be as much as a full meal. It seemed quite unfair to me. We were not busy, it was not a difficult task, and the ingredients were cheap. So I charged the customer what I thought was a fair price, less than half what the owner had said. A small act of rebellion.

I spent the summer between school and university working as a mouse technician in a scientific laboratory doing genetics research. I provided cover for the technicians who were on holiday and my work was varied and interesting. I earned seven pounds and ten shillings a week, and some of that went on bus fares and lunches. It confirmed my interest in genetics,

Last day at school, burning our hats. I am front right wearing a white headband.

and at that time I saw scientific research as my future career.

The lab I worked in was investigating the inheritance of coat colour, and the mice were killed and their skins dried and examined. One day a mouse escaped while a technician was handling it and it ran across the windowsill and jumped out of the open window. We were on the first floor, but the mouse landed and quickly ran off. I was rather sad when it was recaptured and returned to its cage. The animals were well cared for and were killed humanely, and it did not concern me at the time. Now I wonder why I did not question it. It was not a vivisection lab, although there had been protests because it kept animals in cages. The manager explained that these mice were bred and slaughtered as part of a scientific experiment, so it was not really different from farming animals for food, although a mink farm would have been a closer analogy.

The school persuaded me to take the Oxbridge entrance exams, and I was invited to both Oxford (St Hugh's) and Cambridge (Girton) for interviews and practical exams during a very cold winter. I do not know what I expected but even though I was offered a waiting list place at Oxford, it would not have suited me at all. Most candidates were from public schools, were clearly well-off and knew each other. I felt like a real outsider and I was not at all sure that I would have liked being an insider. The accommodation was cold and draughty, and I was glad I had packed my hot water bottle. But I was mortified when it burst in the middle of the night, soaking the bedclothes. I slept on top of a towel and left a note for the cleaner explaining that the wetness was only due to water. I noticed that my bed socks, which had been wet had vanished, but they reappeared the next day, washed and dried.

When I was interviewed at Exeter University I immediately felt more at home. I was embarrassed when Professor Harvey asked me why I did not want to study medicine. I replied that I did not think I would have enough "patience", then realised that he could have thought I said I would not have enough "patients".

However, I was accepted and I loved it there. My parents decided it was time to get a telephone, although it was a party line with the bungalow next door and the two households always seemed to want to use the phone at the same time. I was so lucky that higher education was free back then. I received a full grant from the local education au-

Me, aged 17, with Mum and Dad.

thority that covered my fees, living costs and travel. Students today build up crippling debts.

Chapter Two

Student Days

The University of Exeter

When I went to Exeter University in 1963 there were only 3,000 students there. My degree was in science, but it was also my introduction to the appreciation of classical music, drama and art. I socialised most nights, usually until well after midnight, yet I never missed a 9am lecture. A regular treat with my friend Sarah was to go out to dinner to the Ship Inn near the cathedral. We always started the meal with a schooner of sweet sherry and then tucked into a prawn cocktail, steak and chips, and ice cream. It cost, I think, seven shillings and eleven pence for a three-course meal, and we felt oh so sophisticated.

I had applied for a place in a hall of residence but building delays meant this was not possible until my second year. The university provided a list of approved lodgings, so with another three first year students we went to a house about fifteen minutes' walk from the campus. I also had to share a room, which was hard. The first few days were fine, then we realised how dirty the place was and how unappetising the food. The landlady was ill, and her family were no help. We had to fend for ourselves and soon realised we needed new digs. We spent most evenings of that first term looking for new accommodation. My friend David was now at Exeter Tech and his parents lived in Exmouth, a few miles down the coast. I spent several weekends visiting them, relishing good food and company and alleviating the homesickness. David's father worked on the local newspaper and saw an advert from a new landlady looking for students. He told us about it before it appeared in the press, and we were delighted with our new home. We had to get it approved but that was a formality and we moved in after Christmas.

I took an honours degree in zoology and I loved the frequent field trips to the coast and Dartmoor. The Biological Society was very active and I became the secretary – partly, I have to admit, to get my name in the university diary. We invited prestigious biologists to speak and the chairman and I had to take them out to dinner. One of our members had the idea of trying to educate the general public about nature and with the full support of the biology departments we staged a

Zoology and Botany staff and students. I am far right in the second row.

week-long exhibition called a "conversazione". We worked in small teams to create exhibits which ranged widely. There was an impressive display of flowers from Australia with the centrepiece being two large cones of native flowers encased in ice. We had animals changing colour against different backgrounds. We learned how to take, develop and mount photographs. The local press and radio advertised our initiative enthusiastically. Looking back, I realise how impressive it was that the university allowed us to take a week out of the teaching timetable. They provided practical advice and materials, and we learned far more than with the traditional teaching methods.

I did a science degree so we did not have to wear our gowns to lectures, but females could not wear trousers and males needed a tie. On one occasion the professor of botany followed a student into the lecture hall and, noting the long hair, said "Miss, you cannot wear jeans to my lecture." The student turned, revealing a long beard and an open-necked shirt. The professor, unfazed, said "In your case, you need to wear a tie." And the student was not allowed in.

The structure of the degree was three years of your honours subject (zoology in my case), two years of an additional subject – botany – and one year of a subsidiary subject: psychology. We carried out a psychology project in pairs in class and then had to write it up over the Christmas holidays. I passed the assignment but was angered by a comment on my script which said my account was very similar to the one submitted by my partner. The implication was that I or she had cheated. We had not compared notes at all, and I would not cheat. Apart from the unfairness, we used the same data which we had collected together, so our accounts were bound to be similar. Nowadays I would ask to discuss the matter with the lecturer.

All science students were required to have an "O" Level or equivalent in two languages. Like most of my class-mates, I only had French as my school did not offer any other modern languages. I thought it was unfair they did not accept Latin, one of my favourite subjects, as it is a very useful ety-mological base. So this meant we had to take and pass a course in scientific German run by the university. The classes were boring, with no clear structure. I remember one exercise when I translated a "domestic hen" as a "chicken house"! I had little enthusiasm other than to pass the exam, which fortunately allowed the use of a dictionary so I scraped through.

At the end of our first term we had a botany exam. I failed it, and was mortified to receive a letter from the profes-sor saying that if my performance did not improve my studies would be terminated. I had worked hard, and I had never failed an exam at school. I was slightly relieved when I found out that everyone else had failed too. Several months later I was told that failing all students was a deliberate tactic to en-courage us to work harder, but I felt it was cruel and unneces-sary and it dented the confidence of many of us. Nowadays I hope I would challenge such a practice, but then I was young and shy and I have always found it easier to complain on be-half of someone else than to stand up for my own rights.

I was delighted to move into hall for my second and third years and to have a single room. There was a formal dinner every Thursday, and we were expected to wear an academic gown over sober clothes. In my induction letter I was told to purchase a grey long-sleeved dress for formal meals. I did so, but I soon realised that most students dressed more casually. Indeed, one summer a girl came to dinner wearing her gown over a bikini!

We loved formal dances and spent hours making our own dresses in the sewing room. The summer ball was the event of the year. One year we entered through a waterfall. This was a

Summer Ball, 1964.

framework from floor to ceiling covered in flowers and ferns with water pouring down on either side of a bower. We walked across a wooden bridge over a small stream. This became quite slippery from the spray, but health and safety risk assessments seemed irrelevant back then. We had several rooms for dancing: with the Animals playing pop in one and Vic Oliver in another for ballroom dancing. We had a lavish meal, danced all night and had breakfast at 5am.

There was a focus on environmental practical work and there were three week-long field trips. In the first year, we spent a week under canvas in Dartmoor. One of our field experiments was to estimate the grasshopper population by the capture/release/recapture method. We captured all the grasshoppers in a measured area of grassland. We marked the underside of their abdomens with harmless red nail varnish and released them. A couple of days later we captured all the grasshoppers in the same area and identified how many were marked with the varnish. The way we collected the creatures was using a vacuum cleaner which sucked them up through a wide nozzle. The method worked, but we got some very strange looks from tourists who wondered why we were trying to clean the moorland.

One evening one of the lecturers offered to take me and three other students on a trip to Chesil Beach. We piled into his minivan and reached the reed beds at dusk. We walked through the tall reeds which were way over our heads and got a little lost. Eventually we emerged onto the beach and rushed into the sea, splashing water all over our jeans. When we returned to the van, the lecturer realised he had very little fuel and the petrol stations would be closed. So we slept in the van until 7am, when the garage in the nearest village opened. He filled up and drove back to camp, and no-one had even missed us.

The field trip in year two was to the Scilly Isles where our professor had a holiday home, near to that of the Prime Minister, Harold Wilson. The staff travelled by helicopter, but the students went by the ferry, known as "Vomiting Venus" due to the unfortunate rolling as it hit the Gulf Stream. Once we had regained our equilibrium we had a wonderful time. The weather was balmy, and we went to a different island each day to explore the flora and fauna. No-one suffered from seasickness on the small boats for our

Collecting butterflies on Dartmoor, taken by Tuppy Owens who became a famous photographer.

daily trips.

In my final year we went on a field trip to Sète in the South of France. This was paid by my grant as it was a course requirement. The journey involved two overnight train journeys each way (Exeter-London and Paris-Marseilles), sitting up in a crowded carriage. We went to a field station of the University of Montpelier on the Mediterranean. We dined in cafés near the harbour. Fishermen came into the cafés with their catch and we ate it. I vividly remember the trip back through France. We were bleary-eyed, drinking cheap wine and eager for news of the election at home. At each station we checked newspapers and became elated as the Labour victory became more likely. Most students were left wing and were delighted with the landslide win by Labour and Harold Wilson in March 1966.

Cliffs in Sète, taken by Tuppy Owens.

The zoology professor's wife also worked in the department as a researcher. She had two very different academic interests. One was seaweed, and she could often be seen on the beach with a large red bucket collecting specimens. Her other topic was human fertility and I remember an often-told anecdote. She was interviewing people to join her team as an assistant. She explained the research to one teenage girl and

Keith, the lecturer in the office next door, could hear every word. At one point she asked the girl if she "had ever seen a male sex organ" and immediately followed it with a loud call "Keith. Are you there?" He replied rather hesitantly, and he was so relieved when she simply said, "Put the kettle on."

In spite of my love for nature, my focus became more on biochemistry, cell biology and genetics. I was the only student who chose genetics as my special subject for my final practical exam. My task was to set up a cell culture experiment, which meant wearing protective clothing and a mask and being observed. I found this quite embarrassing as everyone else in the room was doing dissection without being watched. This seemed unfair, as I was being judged on a process as well as an outcome while the rest of the class were assessed only on the final product at the end of the exam. At the time I just felt uncomfortable, but now I regard it as a poor choice of assessment method.

Our degree results were posted on an open noticeboard which was great if you were successful, but excruciating if you had to receive your failure in front of your friends. I remember one student who was so worried he said he thought they might "take my A Levels away." Another girl was quite content to receive a Desmond (a 2.2, named after Archbishop Tutu), but was distressed that no one congratulated her on her degree. Giving results to the recipients privately is a real step forward.

I decided I wanted to do a PhD in genetics and applied to Edinburgh University. I had never been to Scotland and it was a long way away, but it was the obvious choice and I did not apply anywhere else. However, my acceptance depended on getting a good degree so I also started looking for a job. Firms came to the campus for preliminary interviews and then invited promising candidates to their headquarters. One of my second interviews was with Pfizer (well-known now for developing a vaccine against Covid-19) based in Sandwich in Kent. They paid my travel expenses and put me up in the Kings Arms; the first time I had stayed in a good hotel. I had a lovely dinner of gammon and pine-apple and met someone who had just started work for the firm. He explained that they paid for a few weeks in the hotel when you joined.

BSc (Hons.) graduation photo.

The tour round the Pfizer labs was fascinating, and the interview went well. I genuinely cannot remember if they offered me a job or if I would have wanted it. I was keen to explain that I really wanted to do a doctorate before getting a job. They asked if I knew the area and I ex-plained that I had been born in Margate, about ten miles away. When they realised my grandparents still lived there, a driver in a posh car took me on a surprise visit. They were delighted to see me, although I could only stay a few hours before getting the train back to Exeter.

The University of Edinburgh

Just before my twenty-first birthday I arrived at the Universi-ty of Edinburgh to do my PhD in genetics. I have some Scottish blood on my paternal grandmother's side, and I fell in love with Scotland. Edinburgh is a beautiful city with a vibrant culture and easy access to wonderful countryside. Even within the city I regularly walked up Arthur's Seat to enjoy views across the city and the River Forth. I lived in the newly-built Pollock Halls of Residence on Dalkeith Road. This was a complex of half a dozen blocks, served by a central refectory and social area. Until the previous year, men were only allowed in female student rooms on Sunday afternoon, but by 1966 men were allowed in bedrooms until 9pm. A few years earlier in other universities, the bedroom doors always had to be open when entertaining the opposite sex. There was no official suggestion then of same-sex romantic relationships. By the time I left in 1969, if you had an overnight guest for more than two nights you were asked to pay for their meals.

The study bedrooms all had a washbasin, but none had toilets or showers. As a postgrad I had my own kitchen with a small fridge and a Baby Belling cooker. The other postgrad in Baird House was an Indian lady doing a PhD about the Irish writer Yeats, and we became firm friends. Gowrie lent me an embroidered silk sari to wear to a party. I looked very glamorous but I spent the whole night worrying that the garment might fall off. I was also a sub-warden, which meant a reduction in the rent. My pastoral duties were limited and mostly consisted of replacing light bulbs when I was on duty. In vacation times only the PhD students remained in the complex. There were about thirty of us across half a dozen houses from all over the world. The halls were rented out as holiday accommodation, and a Scottish aspect was added by having a piper play at 8 o'clock every morning. This may have delighted the visitors, but we soon got fed up with it.

I was based in the Institute of Animal Genetics at Kings Buildings. Again I had a full grant, this time from the Medical Research Council due to a somewhat spurious link with human eye conditions. The department was a friendly place. Friday lunch was always in a local pub, and there were plenty of parties. There was a common room and cafeteria on campus, and as I walked in one day to watch a bit of Wimbledon on television I was amazed to see green grass courts. It was my first sight of colour TV. One international student whose grant had run out was supported unofficially until he could complete his PhD. Staff brought him in food, there were showers in the building, and he slept on a bench in the CT (constant temperature) room that housed some key experiments. Some years previously many of the staff had lived together in communal style at Mortonhall House. Apparently this eventually failed as there was tension between different factions of staff. The experiences were turned into a thinly disguised novel called *The Last Masters* (1953) by Edith Simon, who was married to a member of staff.

My first year was occupied with a Postgraduate Diploma in Animal Genetics with lectures, seminars and practical work. I saw an overhead projector for the first time. It was a revelation as the lecturer could face us while writing on the screen, unlike the blackboard. Also transparencies could be prepared beforehand and used later for revision. I was so impressed with this modern technology. We were assessed by essays and exams. One of my essays was apparently very good and the marker wanted to give it 100%. She was told this was not appropriate as any essay had some subjective aspects and there was always the possibility that someone could have done it better. The diploma was not graded, but I was told that my performance was at the level of first-class degree.

My research into the biochemical systems operating in the eyes of toads was part of a collection of related projects being carried out by the "Lens Group". This group of three academics, three technicians and five research students became my academic family. The atmosphere was supportive and the work was intellectually challenging, but I soon felt that I was not cut out for a career in research. It seemed too lonely and too convergently focused. As this realisation took hold I was upset, as doing genetics research had been my ambition for the previous seven years.

Like most doctoral students, I worked a few hours a week as a demonstrator, helping first year students with practical classes. The extra money was handy, and I found I really enjoyed these sessions. I got to know my students, and they began to talk to me about more than the cockroach they were dissecting. I remember one student who returned after Christmas with terrible burns on the back of his hand. In a drunken state he had branded himself with a cigarette with the initials of his current girlfriend, and the wounds has become infected. He assured me it was not painful but I encouraged him to seek medical attention, and I was pleased that he seemed to regret his actions. A few of the students explained that they were confused about some of the lecture content, so I arranged to borrow some educational films which explained the key points. I showed these to them in optional sessions after the practical classes and they became quite popular. I soon realised that this was my favourite part of the week. I really enjoyed helping the students understand the subject. I began to identify their learning needs and to find ways to meet them.

Professor Waddington, who was head of Animal Genetics, had wide-ranging interests and the department library had a section on biological education. I spotted an advert for a research fellow in biology and education at Glasgow University. This was a momentous stroke of luck that changed my career direction dramatically. I applied and was amazed to get the job, due – I was told – to my enthusiasm. I took up the post and moved into a shared flat in Glasgow.

I had only completed two years of my PhD, and everyone said if I left then I would never finish it. That was just the spur I needed. I spent the first year focusing on my new job and then completed my doctorate. I worked for Glasgow during the day, had dinner in the staff club, and worked on my thesis in the evenings. At weekends I returned to Edinburgh to continue with some experimental work and stayed with various friends. At last it was finished and bound in black leather with the title *Biochemical Studies of Induction and Development of the Vertebrate Lens* emblazoned in gold. Back then the thesis had to be bound before submission; later students would submit a soft bound copy for the viva exam which could be modified before final binding. Nowadays theses only exist in electronic form, and it is hard work when you have to read them as an examiner. I found my viva very stressful, but it was successful and I was delighted that the external said that it was well written. I only had to make minor changes to one page, so I retyped that page and sliced out the old one with a Stanley knife and stuck the new page in. It saved the expense of rebinding. Years later I debated the purpose of a PhD. Was it about the process of learning about research methodology, or about the product – i.e. the findings from the study?

The ideal applicant for the Glasgow job needed to know about individualised learning, self-assessment methods, the design of learning materials using different media, and evaluation – as well as biology. That person needed a post-graduate diploma in educational technology, and such a course did not exist back then. But seven years later I was running the DipEdTech programme in Dundee.

Part 2:
My Living

Chapter Three

The University of Glasgow

The Biology Teaching Project

My job in Glasgow was part of the Inter-University Biology Teaching Project financed by the Nuffield Foundation in five universities. It was led by Professor "Bunny" Dowdeswell, whom I had met at Juniper Hall. He wrote about the project and said "One of the outstanding features of the enterprise is that it seeks to combine biological expertise with educational technology... In addition to aiding understanding and learning, we hope the use of self-instruction will achieve a saving in time and manpower". In practice, self-instruction often increases learning and may lead to timesaving for some students, but staff are still needed with a different role. Instead of lecturing, the academics design materials but then ideally provide tutorial support. The project provided self-assessment so students could measure their own progress, though I now think that the presence of a tutor would have enhanced the educational experience. But hindsight is easy.

It was a temporary post for three years, although it was extended to six years. The salary was excellent. As a research fellow I received £1,800 p.a. at a time when a research assistant or assistant lecturer was on only £1,100 p.a. This meant that after a couple of years I was able to buy a flat in Hyndland Road, about fifteen minutes' walk from the university. The flat had three bedrooms and a large lounge with high ceilings and beautiful decorated cornices. It cost £8,300 and I sold it four years later for £12,000!

My appointment was jointly in the departments of zoology and education, and my office was located within education. At first this felt strange, as my background was in science which was part of my professional identity. I even insisted on having a Bunsen burner in my office, although I only ever used it to boil water for coffee. The education department was small and very friendly and I soon felt at home, and my metamorphosis into a new discipline was painless. My colleagues, knowing I was a biologist, set about explaining key educational ideas to me. These are still relevant, although they have been refined over time:

- Curriculum alignment ensured that learning objectives, teaching methods and assessment worked together. If, for instance, you are learning to drive you must be taught and be assessed in a practical manner, although this can be underpinned by theoretical learning.
- Learning objectives have a hierarchy. Knowledge and comprehension are low level objectives, but they need to be mastered before the student can tackle higher order objectives such as analysis and synthesis.
- Students learn in different ways. Teachers should encourage them to explore what works for them. Offering a range of teaching methods is an equitable way to provide learning opportunities for students with differ-

ent needs and interests. The individualised learning approach used in the project fitted well with this, and allowed students to choose some aspects of their mode of study.

- There is another hierarchy that suggests that basic needs must be met before higher ones. Students do not learn well if they are hungry or tired, so build in breaks to learning. A sense of self-esteem is important, so treat students with respect and ensure peer pressure is supportive not bullying. These basic needs will allow a student to reach their full potential.

I also had to develop some managerial skills. I was responsible for budgets, reports and a small team of photographers, graphics artists and a secretary. We had 800 first year students studying biology, and half of them had not studied the basics of the subject at school. We designed a couple of bridge courses to bring them up to speed. The students took a diagnostic multiple-choice test to identify specific gaps in their biological knowledge. We were them able to give each student a personalised list of programmes to study at their own pace. We produced two suites of programmes: *The Biology of Development* (15 programmes) and *The Behaviour of Animals* (10 programmes), affectionately known as "Bod" and "Boa". Each programme contained a set of slides (or filmstrip), an audio cassette and a workbook. Biology is a very visual subject and I soon learned to ensure the audio and visual channels complemented each other, as well as providing a good resource for students with different learning styles. We also wrote a teacher's guide, as the packages were to be sold to other institutions.

The programmes had several advantages, as I explained in the advertising material:

- **Learner-controlled**: The student has control over their own learning. They can take as much time as they need, and can replay parts if required. They can be used with students with mixed academic backgrounds.
- **Relevant responding**: Questions focus on key points and maintain attention. The student receives feedback on their progress.
- **Multimedia**: Each channel of communication has its own role, but they interact to complement each other.
- **Workbook retained**: The student has a permanent record for later revision.
- **Post-test**: A multiple choice test can be used by students or teachers to assess learning.
- **Multiple uses**: The programme can be used in a resource centre, or for home study, or for group presentations followed by discussion.

This individualised learning was based on tapes, slides and workbooks – a far cry from the interactive online learning I delivered later in my career. We set up a room with individual study stations and the students booked in. We borrowed an old industrial timeclock from a local shipyard, and the students punched in and out with personal timecards. Although the whole scheme was voluntary, they loved the theatre of clocking in and out – but it did make an awful noise.

Some students found self-study to be lonely, and they lacked the motivation to attend the study centre. When we showed the tape-slide programmes in a lecture room at a set time, a few chose to attend. We gave them the self-study booklets and allowed them to discuss the answers before we moved on to the next slide. This approach was popular with some learners who benefited from the discipline imposed by a timetabled session and also enjoyed learning in groups.

After about a year, the student evaluations proved the value of the project and we set up a self-teaching lab on the top floor of the new Boyd Orr science building. At times it was very busy, and I noticed students waiting in an adjacent space for a slot on the resources. I set up a series of exhibitions on biological themes that changed every few weeks. The topics included plant hormones, heredity, nature conservation, pollution, and animal senses. They were informative and colourful, and included simple activities and experiments as well as handouts to take away. I added some microscopes and microscope slides in addition to some commercial programmes on aspects of biology, and the lab became a popular venue.

There were lots of collaborations involved in the project. A team of biologists worked with me on the content. Audio-visual experts contributed to the design and production. Meetings with other university teams in the project allowed sharing of ideas. One of the venues for our regular meetings was the Royal Society in London, so I was excited to say I have given a lecture at such a prestigious address. I involved students in the piloting of the resources and developed my own skills in evaluation methods. We worked with Longmans to publish and sell the materials to other universities and colleges. I learned a lot about collaboration, cooperation and competition, and the subtle differences between these processes. The different universities vied with each other for personal prestige and possible extra funding. There were some tensions between the educationalists with their theories of learning and the biologists who knew the subject matter and their own students. The final sentence of one of the papers I wrote about the project hints at some of the pressures on the initiative: "Local constraints on implementation are apt to get in the way of education."

I always tried to write and speak with some wit, using metaphors and adding gentle humour to the message. I am not sure this always worked, but I felt that many academic publications were too dry and esoteric. I gave a staff seminar at Glasgow under the title "Plug me in and I'll turn you on." The presentation went well, but in the formal report of all seminars that term, my title seemed very unacademic. The following extract from a chapter I wrote for a Nuffield Foundation book shows my style for whimsy and illustrates the comments I made earlier about collaboration:

> The first-year biology course was run by a consortium of departments. I was employed in just one of them and I came from outside. Some people seemed to regard me as an interloper, trespassing on their territory and poaching their students. My programmes were always intended to be an optional but important extra, but to some staff they remained the trivial decoration on the cake – tasty but not very nutritious. As the offspring of two disciplines (biology and education) I tried to exhibit hybrid vigour. Gradually I became less of a buffer and more of a catalyst between the subject experts and the educational technologists, and a reaction product began to emerge.

The professor of education was a brilliant academic and a delightful person. Every year he held a staff picnic at his holiday house on Loch Long. My colleagues and, I together with their families, boarded a steamer down the loch. Then the professor rowed out to collect us a few at a time in his little dinghy.

He also took his pastoral responsibilities seriously. Receiving a note about checking the fire equipment in the building, he investigated. The main part of the education department was in an old converted house in University Gardens. There was no fire escape from the offices on the top floor, but there was a rope ladder outside the window which would give you access to the balcony below. The professor tried it out. Unfortunately the rope had perished, the ladder broke, and he fell and injured his ankle. When he retired, the University hosted a dinner for him. His many colleagues, ex-students and friends clubbed together to buy him a small sailboat which was installed behind a screen in the refectory and revealed after the meal.

The education department was involved in several collaborative projects, including one on medical education with Ronnie Harden. We shared graphic artists and photographers as well as audio-visual equipment. In the early 1970s, Ronnie moved to Dundee to set up the Centre for Medical Education, maintaining links to Glasgow.

I attended some evening classes run by the education department on programmed learning. This approach is rather rigid, but it introduced me to key ideas such as learning objectives, sequential learning and self-assessment. I enjoyed the course and it was very relevant in my new job. Two years later I was running the course to a collection of teachers and industrial trainers. Each participant had to design and test some programmed learning materials in their own context, so I found myself tutoring on a wide range of topics. These projects were assessed by an external examiner from the City and Guilds, and led to a qualification. This was the first time that I realised that the teachers were assessed as well as the students.

I also ran some education seminars as part of the MEd programme, and my Wednesday evenings became rather frantic. The seminars ran from 4.30 to 6pm, and I rushed down to Byres Road to buy fish and chips which I gobbled down before returning to the department to run my evening class on programmed learning from 7 to 9pm.

At Glasgow University the staff had their own graduation ball. The men wore evening suits with academic gowns and hoods and were accompanied by their female partners in long ball-gowns. There were few female academics then, and we wore a gown and hood over our evening dress to show that we were members of staff in our own right, not partners. It was very hot when dancing the Gay Gordons!

The learning packages were published by Longmans, and the university received the royalties. The project had been popular with the students, so it had been successful in terms of outcome and output. But positive student evaluations were no match for financial matters or internal politics. I had a vain hope that the university might take over the funding of my post, but it was never on the cards. Also, the space occupied by our resources centre in the Boyd Orr Building was under threat from another department. So I needed to find another job – and a permanent one. I had enjoyed my time in Glasgow, and it had given me the opportunity of two overseas trips.

Poland

I travelled to an international conference in Poznan in Poland with a couple of colleagues from the UK. My initial impressions were rather negative, as this extract from my journal shows:

> I stagger out of the carriage, clutching my suitcase. I am stiff and tired after travelling for twelve hours by air to Warsaw and then rail to Poznan. I follow my colleagues through an underpass and we move forward with the crowds and then stop abruptly. The station is flooded due to a torrential downpour that has burst the drains. In front of us is a river of muddy water about ten feet across. It is the only way out so we step into the swirling water which is ankle deep and very cold. When we reach the concourse it is still pouring and no taxis are evident. Fortunately the hotel is only a few blocks away, but when we arrive, cold and bedraggled, we are too late for a hot meal, and soggy sandwiches are the only option. I wash my sodden shoes with shampoo, dry them with toilet paper and put them on the radiator. After a good sleep and a delicious breakfast, I put on my surprisingly wearable shoes and walk the short distance to Poznan University of Technology. It is a beautiful September morning and I now feel positive about my visit to Poland.

I gave a paper on aspects of visual communication and was paid by the number of words in my paper. Some months before, I had asked a graphic artist on my project to draw a fly as part of a life cycle diagram. He examined a dead fly under a microscope and produced a very detailed drawing showing every hair on the fly's body. But what I wanted was a simple line drawing, as the detail was distracting. In my presentation I illustrated the idea of "frog" with a series of slides showing a colour photograph, a black and white photo, a detailed coloured drawing, a simple line drawing, a cartoon, and the word FROG. When the next slide showed the Polish word for frog (ŻABA), the audience clapped and cheered. I also mounted an exhibition with some examples of the materials I had produced, including a filmstrip, an audio tape and a workbook. By the second day, the tape and workbook had been taken and the filmstrip had been cut into sections, leaving just the ends. I was told by a local that his colleagues were so desperate for "Western" examples that even a fragment was valuable.

It was not all work. The conference dinner was lavish and included a bottle of vodka between every four delegates. Our travel package included tickets to the opera and hearing "Aida" sung in Polish was very strange. We were accommodated in a good hotel, but we were turned out on the final night as all the hotels had given preferential treatment to those involved in the international trade fair. We were all moved into student accommodation, which was dire. I felt really sorry for the students who had to endure a room with curtains so thin they were almost see-through and a sink so badly cracked that it could only hold an inch of water before it poured onto the floor. By way of compensation, we were given free entry to the trade fair which was fascinating with a lively carnival atmosphere.

We also had a day in Krakow, a beautiful old city. I bought a tiny vase filled with artificial flowers as a memento in a tourist shop. The people were friendly, but somehow subdued. This was just a few years before the Solidarity trade union developed into a campaign against the communist regime. Drinking tea in the city square, we heard an unfinished bugle tune and were told this related to the Mongolian invaders in 1241. A lone sentry spotted their advance and blew his bugle from St Mary's Church tower. This alerted the townsfolk and the Mongolians were forced to retire. But not before they had fired arrows at the sentry and killed him in the midst of his warning. I was moved by the story, and wrote this poem in the plane on the way home:

> Dried flowers in a blue vase.
> Papery memories,
> Permanent but inferior.
> We cling to past joys.
> We vicariously live again,
> Safe in the knowledge
> We cannot suffer,
> We cannot fail,
> We cannot die.
> People cling to their religion,
> Desperately faithful,
> Afraid to believe they no longer own their country.
> Inwardly proud and sad.
> Still the defiant bugle plays,
> Ceasing abruptly

I still have the little blue vase, though the dried flowers disintegrated some time ago. I also purchased a bottle of slivovitz, but it tasted awful and it ended up in the water bottle in my car as a de-icer. It was effective, but the alcoholic fumes were rather overwhelming.

The United States of America and Canada

I had a two-week trip to Canada and the USA, paid for by the Carnegie Foundation and the Scottish Education Department. My Dad, feeling protective, offered to come with me and although I felt mean at denying him the opportunity, I realised that this was something I had to do on my own. For years after, when my confidence and self-assurance wavered I was sustained by memories of my successful trip across the pond.

It was my first intercontinental flight, and I was entranced by the in-flight movies and the wonderful food. I flew into New York for a connection to Atlanta, but my destination was fog-bound and flights were delayed for five hours. New York was not part of my itinerary, but I could not waste the opportunity. The weather there was a bright and clear November day. I asked a member of airport staff where I could get a bus into the city. After he gave me a timetable, he explained that I should not talk to strangers or go away from the main thoroughfares. I felt quite touched by his concern and wondered if I would need to report back when I returned for my onward flight. I had a lovely time on my bonus visit and went up the Empire State Building with visibility at 25 miles.

I attended a conference in Atlanta, Georgia – an interesting event and a fascinating city. I wanted to visit Stone Mountain to see the carvings of the Confederate figures Jefferson Davies, Stonewall Jackson and Robert E. Lee. The only way I could get there was by bus, which trundled through the poor suburbs of the city. I was the only white person on the bus and, although I attracted a few puzzled looks, everyone was polite.

After the conference I began a short study tour to eight colleges and universities in America and Canada that were delivering courses using self-instructional packages. This individualised learning approach allowed students to study at their own pace using interactive learning materials rather than attending mass lectures. I learned about the systems, talked to the staff and students, and gave a few seminars about my own work. The audiences were impressed by the quality of the Glasgow materials and were intrigued that they were an additional feature, not a replacement of the traditional lecture courses.

The "Audio Tutorial", or AT approach, included clear objectives, audio guides to structured resources, and frequent quizzes. There was also a great deal of support from the lecturers on an individual tailored basis. This was the most significant difference from our self-teaching lab, which was unstaffed. In several institutions, the AT approach led to higher scores in exams and thus to increased popularity of the scheme. However, this sometimes had a negative backlash. A high grade in AT measures the students against assessment criteria, not against their peers. But entry into advanced courses is selective, so some students at Cornell University chose the traditional mode of study since an "A" achieved that way was accepted as a discriminator of high ability. In another university, the biggest problem seemed to be that the students scored too well. At the University of Toronto, the central administration did not know how to compare criterion-referenced grades from AT courses with the norm-referenced scores from other subjects. Apart from higher grades, the students who used the AT method developed improved study habits including problem solving, time management, and the ability to find and organise information. At Purdue University, advanced students of botany were required to produce an AT mini-course about a plant of their own choice. They received individual advice from staff, but the design was theirs. They learned photography and presentation skills as well as plant anatomy. Fellow students accessed the mini-courses to learn the content and they also provided evaluative comments.

One of the most extreme forms of AT was at the medical School in McMaster University in Hamilton, Ontario, and I felt it had gone too far in the direction of student freedom. The students chose their own route through resources, which might be concerning for future patients. Would you want to be treated by a doctor who had chosen to omit some systems in the body? The study packages were not interactive, with no self-assessment to measure progress. However, I liked the problem box idea where students worked through case studies based on real patient data and discussed ideas in tutorials.

I was struck by the enthusiasm of the lecturers involved and I wondered how much of the success was due to their passion and charisma. If the key innovator left, would the project founder? They were, after all, "projects" and had not been institutionalised. I have been an advocate of blended learning and self-paced study for many years, but it has taken a pandemic for it to become the accepted mode of education.

As I flew from Atlanta north to New York and then Canada, I watched the progression of the seasons as the autumnal colours moved to ice and snow. This was November. I stayed in a hotel in Buffalo and enquired about visiting Niagara Falls. There were several Japanese tourists staying there too, so the hotel arranged for a cab to take me and four others on a trip. When we reached the falls, the driver stopped frequently so we could take photos. But it soon became apparent that we were expected to experience this dramatic spectacle through the cab windows alone. After half an hour I asked him to drop me off and said I would make my own way back. I donned the oilskins provided and went down behind the falls, getting drenched by the spray and deafened by the noise. Then I walked across to the American side and explored there. Eventually I caught a bus back to the hotel, having had a wonderful day.

Everyone I met was welcoming and friendly. I was wined and dined, and often given free accommodation in university houses or halls of residence. I went to a breakfast meeting and was presented with a stack of pancakes about ten inches tall. (I only managed to eat a quarter of them.) I was invited to the family home of a lecturer to join the celebrations for his mother, who had arrived from Greece a few years earlier and had just achieved her American citizenship. Even strangers were helpful and outgoing. When I flew back to the UK, I changed planes at London for Glasgow. As all the passengers studiously avoided me and each other, I realised I was back home.

I wrote reports for my sponsors, and they have proved useful now to remind me of my experiences nearly half a century later. This is the final paragraph of my Carnegie Report:

When the AT system works well, it is excellent. As a direct result of it more students achieve better marks. I was impressed by the enthusiasm of the staff and the students. The students soon learn to work well on their own and become very good at problem solving, designing experiments and interpreting data. This is even true of school children in their early teens. Cooperation rather than competition between students is encouraged and seems to make a positive contribution to the success of the system. But perhaps the most significant factor in determining the success or failure of an AT course is the tutor in charge.

In the mid-1990s I received a request from the Carnegie Foundation to review a research application. It was quite bulky, so I took it with me on a train journey for a meeting in Edinburgh. I knew the applicant from another university slightly, and I was surprised to see him sitting further down the carriage. My initial thought was that he was a hallucination that I had conjured up, but he was real. We exchanged pleasantries, but I did not explain what I was reading since reviews were confidential.

My report for the SED was much more detailed, with an account of every centre I visited. My final paragraph was prescient, as it described exactly what I was doing some years later in Dundee:

I am now full of enthusiasm to try a pilot of an AT scheme here. I am convinced it could work. I would like to try to teach part of a course not with the three Ls – lectures, labs and library books – but with a resource based independent learning system which is available, individualised, interactive and self-paced. I had a wonderful time. I returned physically exhausted but mentally refreshed and exhilarated.

Educational Technology

This was an exciting time to be involved in education, full of change and innovation. The concept of educational technology was not just about computers and videos, but about a systematic approach to curriculum design. There was a shift in focus from teaching to learning, and a move to give the students more autonomy. We now talk about learning outcomes routinely, but back then the idea of stating objectives was novel. To build the teaching around what you expected the learner to be able to do by the end had major implications. The objectives acted as a blueprint to help you plan the content, the method of teaching and ways to assess their achievement. The ideas were controversial. Some felt they made education too rigid, denying the teacher's creativity. Others said in horror that if you told the students what the objectives were, they might all meet them!

A group of like-minded educators formed an informal organisation called the Glasgow and West of Scotland Programmed Learning Group (known as Gooseplug). We were interested in individualised learning methods and the use of technology to facilitate and enhance teaching. We soon changed our name to the West of Scotland Educational Technology Group (or WedTech). We had a few members from Edinburgh and Dundee, and the focus was always on the education – not the technology. We ran an annual conference. I was a keen member, and was soon elected to the organising committee. We worked hard planning events that were popular, innovative and cheap. Many of the conferences were held in colleges during vacation, and we often had access to a games room. A popular activity after the conference dinner was a form of table tennis with two bats and about thirty players. Each person hit the ball and dropped the bat and ran round to the other side of the table where someone hit it back with the second bat. The next person picked up the first bat to return the ball and so on. Anyone who missed a shot was eliminated. It was great fun, especially after a few drinks.

The idea of open learning was growing. The Open University started in 1963 accepting students without the normal entry requirements and allowing them to study at their own pace in their own home. Distance learning was not just about the physical remoteness of the student from the institution, but about the philosophy of individualised study, giving students control over the manner of their education. In this regard, the OU had fairly rigid regulations so it was nick-named the "Slightly Ajar University".

After six years, the biology project in Glasgow was completed. My initial contract was for three years, but this was extended a couple of times. Each time, before it was re-newed, I had to look for a job which was very stressful. Late in 1974 I applied successfully for a post in Dundee. When I left Glasgow in 1975, I was treated to three farewell parties – by zoology, by education, and by the local members of WedTech.

Chapter Four

Dundee College of Education

John Clarke was well known within the Scottish EdTech scene. He was head of the Learning Resources Department which included a print unit and video production team, and he designed a resource centre for the new building of Dundee College of Education. John designed carrels kitted out for different media for individual study. Staff from all departments were supported to design self-study materials using print, audio tape, slides, filmstrips and video. The materials had stated learning objectives, self-tests and assignments. Students worked at their own pace, assessing their own learning. Class tutorials were able to focus on deeper understanding, as the students had covered the basic content on their own. This is the principle underlying blended learning which is now so popular.

The college planned to offer a qualification in EdTech and advertised for a programme leader. My contract at Glasgow was about to end, finally, so I applied. I was invited for interview on Christmas Eve, but I had already booked a flight down to London to visit my parents for the holiday. Dundee agreed to interview me in early January. Since all the other interviewees had all been seen a couple of weeks earlier they said they would make their decision within two hours. So I went into town, not feeling hopeful, and hit the January sales, then returned to the College to hear my

John's carrels in the Learning Resources Centre.

fate. I was offered the job and immediately said that I had just bought a dress because I thought I had failed. They smiled.

I think John's voice was important in my appointment, as I had known him for several years through WedTech meetings. Of course he had no way of knowing that I would end up married to his stepson, Andy. This is an extract from John's autobiography, written in 2014:

I had got to know well many academics in the field of educational technology especially several working in the University of Glasgow. One of these was a Dr Gaye Manwaring with a PhD in biology but a devotee of structured and individualised learning. I knew her to be a highly intelligent, hard-working, creative, trustworthy researcher, thoroughly reliable to carry out her allotted tasks. At her interview, she was not without other very strong and well qualified candidates for the post but I knew whom I wanted and was not to be over-ruled when decision time came. My choice has well justified, her appointment becoming one of Scotland's supremely well experienced and qualified staff in the development of educational practices which were to develop out of the initial, faltering steps of individualised learning and educational technology. Gaye is happily married to Andrew and, now, a semi-retired member of the staff of Dundee University which absorbed the College when all major teacher training courses became of degree standard.

The new job was a permanent appointment as a senior lecturer, and I started work in the spring of 1975. I felt this was really the start of my career in HE. The college was in the middle of salary negotiations and they were unable to tell me how much I would receive. They were annoyed when I refused to sign my contract until I knew. It turned out to be generous, so I was able to achieve one of my ambitions – to earn £3,000 p.a. by the time I was thirty.

I arrived on my first day and walked up the imposing steps at the front of the main building where I had been interviewed. It was situated in Park Place, in what is now the Scrimgeour Building of the University of Dundee. John met me and took me to the learning resources department. We walked through the building and out the back into a muddy car park which contained two large portacabins. The date was the first of April and I wondered if this was a joke, but no. One cabin housed the audiovisual and printing technicians, and we went into the other via some rickety steps. There were several large rooms and the LR office was for John, me, another academic and two secretaries. I was given a desk and some stationery, and my first task which was to outline the structure of the proposed course on EdTech.

Two typewriters clacked away as I tried to focus my attention on what I was writing. They were annoying, but I was getting used to them. Suddenly a new sound – a piano tuning up. I looked up in surprise, but no one else was concerned.

"What's that?" I asked.

John replied: "The Music Department is next door."

"Which side?"

"Both!" he laughed.

Sure enough, from the other side I could hear female voices reciting "Frère Jacques". What with the noise and the smell from three cigarette smokers, I wondered why I had come to Dundee and how I could function effectively? Fortunately it was only for three months, and then the College moved into a new purpose-built home. Until then we were entertained by renditions of "Nymphs and Shepherds" with annoying regularity.

One of the characters was the college doctor, who was rather obsessive about her named parking place. On my second day, someone had parked in her place. She assumed it was me as I was the new member of staff, so she phoned me up and told me angrily to move my car immediately. I was somewhat taken aback as I did not own a car at that time. I was later told about another occasion when someone had the temerity to park in her place. She parked her car in front of the offending vehicle thus blocking it in. The owner gathered some strong friends who physically moved her car so that he could retrieve his vehicle. Then, as a joke, he took his spare wheel, rubbed it in the mud and rolled it over the top of her car as if he had driven over it to escape.

I was told another story about the college doctor. She ran first aid classes for community education students, and taught them how to carry a person on a makeshift stretcher. She chose to be the patient herself and gave instructions about how to secure her rather large body. Once she was firmly strapped in, the students went off for a coffee break, leaving her high and dry.

Professor Ronnie Harden had been a colleague in Glasgow and he invited me to contribute to his courses in the Centre for Medical Education. They attracted participants from all over the world, and I loved running workshops on designing educational materials and assessing students. This was the first teaching I did in Dundee. Ronnie arranged for me to become an Honorary Lecturer at the University of Dundee, presaging my role after retirement. This also allowed me to become a sub-warden in Airlie Hall of Residence and receive free accommodation while I looked for somewhere to buy. The duties were minimal, although we did invite a small number of students for sherry on Thursdays before dinner. One evening a student broke her ankle and I drove her to A&E. Another evening a student knocked on my door to say there was a flood. I followed her and saw water was flowing down the main staircase. Someone had run a bath and then got distracted and the bath had overflowed. I never understood why the student fetched me before turning the taps off and pulling out the plug. Years later Airlie Hall was turned into part of the School of Nursing, and I found myself running educational workshops in what had been student bedrooms.

The college governors had decided that all academic members of staff should be registered with the General Teaching Council for Scotland. Now I would challenge such a suggestion, but this was my first permanent job so I agreed even though I planned never to teach in a school. I had a doctorate, so I was able to qualify as a teacher in a special one term course. I simply had to write two essays and do a four-week teaching practice with two formal observations of my teaching. I went to a local secondary school in Dundee to teach biology. Some of the teachers there were quite rightly upset that I could gain a qualification so easily. It was totally inappropriate, but I explained that it was not my idea and I was never going to use the qualification. Since I did not serve a probationary time in a school I could not get full registration anyway, although I did subsequently gain full GTC registration for further education.

Mostly I was asked to follow the curriculum, but once I was given a free hand and asked to do a lesson on any biological aspect of my choice. I talked about animal behaviour using the content of the learning packages I had developed at Glasgow. This was a great success because I had some attractive slides and introduced the students to some unusual and intriguing examples. I already understood the idea that a good teacher is an "edutainer". While I worked there I confirmed my belief that I did not wish to teach children, and I taught adults, usually mature adults, for the rest of my career.

One bad memory was when another teacher brought two extra pupils into my class, sat them at the side with a textbook and told me just to keep them quiet. They were bored and kept whispering to each other, and I felt angry and frustrated. They were disturbing the class, and I felt the situation was out of my control. I was horrified when I realised I actually wanted to hit them with my ruler. Of course I restrained my urge, but I did consider humiliating them by making fun of them and asking my class to hiss at them for speaking. Again I ignored the idea, but I wondered how other teachers would have handled it. If there had been more room I would have separated them to stop them talking. But I did wonder why they had not been put in the library or given a specific task.

On another occasion I was working with another teacher in charge of the "moddies". This awful name was applied to pupils with special needs who had a modified curriculum and who were often regarded as unruly. We took them to a nearby park and I expected we would be doing a lesson related to nature. But no, the teacher simply got them to run round the flowerbeds. This was to tire them out and keep them out of mischief; learning was not an option. I was appalled. Thankfully some practices have changed for the better.

I had to take a first-year class on sex education using a standard worksheet. I was pleasantly surprised that the pupils were so well behaved. They were interested and curious, but there was no sniggering. They were definitely pre-teens, and I suspect the following year they would have been much harder to manage. I am always keen to help learners relate things to their own experience, but I did not expect personal comments. I had to explain that they should not share intimate details about their families, but not before one boy had told us all that his father had "had the snip", and a girl explained that her mother had found out the hard way that breast feeding is not an effective form of contraception.

I do remember one useful piece of advice from a teacher there. We had a kettle and a toaster in the biology staff room for making lunch. One day I watched him carefully spread butter on his toast. He said there was always plenty of butter in the middle of the slice, so you had to pay attention to the edges. He said it was the same with teaching a class. It was easy to direct your teaching to the middle of the ability range.

But it was essential to cater also for those who struggled who needed extra support, and for the gifted pupils who needed to be challenged.

I do not have children, but I have worked with a lot of schoolteachers. What concerns me is the lack of relevance of the curriculum. It seems over-heavy on knowledge. The Curriculum for Excellence in Scotland wants pupils to be successful learners, confident individuals, responsible citizens, effective contributors – and who could disagree? But these goals are too general, and some people see a political agenda there. I think pupils need to learn about managing money, first aid, changing an electric plug, writing a letter and healthy eating, but I am not sure that all leavers could achieve these aspects. Everyone should learn basic cooking skills, but I can remember two male students when I was at university who had no idea. One used to boil eggs in his electric kettle, until one of the eggs cracked. Another wanted mashed potatoes but tried to mash them before cooking them.

After a few months, the college moved to the campus at Gardyne Road. We held an educational technology conference there the weekend before it was officially occupied. I had the honour of chairing the first session of the first event. Thirty-two years later I organised the final wedding in the chapel for my 85-year-old father, but that is another story. John's wife, Thelma, became the secretary to my course, and I met her son. Andy and I married in 1983 in the college chapel.

Advances in technology allowed computers and multimedia systems to provide a variety of interactive and exciting ways to learn. The Council for Educational Technology (CET) based in London and the Scottish Council for Educational Technology (SCET) in Glasgow were important organisations promoting informational technology and open learning. They ran many projects, and produced a wealth of useful resources. I was heavily involved in both organisations and was on the governing board of SCET. As a thank you, the governors together with their partners were invited to a special reception at Edinburgh Castle. We drank champagne, nibbled delicious canapes and were then given a private viewing of the crown jewels.

One residential meeting was held in the beautiful Creggans Inn in Strachur, on the shore of Loch Fyne. We were asked to put our luggage in our bedrooms but leave the unpacking for later. I was disappointed to be given a tiny room with no window and no bathroom, even though the advance publicity had promised en-suite accommodation. I mentioned it as we assembled for our first meeting, and the organiser was horrified and insisted that I swap rooms with the secretary. I was rather embarrassed, but he assured me it was because I was a voluntary governor and she was a paid employee. I still felt uncomfortable but was pleased with my new room. When I went into my bathroom I found the traditional complimentary pack of soap, shampoo and hand cream. At lunchtime I handed it over to the secretary with an apologetic smile, and she was happy.

On another occasion I travelled to Inverness with the chairman to conduct some interviews for a new project leader. This took a couple of days and, on the train back, we were held up by a landslide at Blair Atholl due to the widening of the A9 road. The train guard said we would be delayed for an hour while the track was cleared of rubble. Then he said the track would take several days to clear and they would send buses to rescue us within a few hours. He offered to make phone calls on behalf of every passenger. So, my husband decided to drive from Dundee to collect me. He found the train abandoned, located my suitcase, and followed the noise to the nearby hotel where all the passengers had decided to wait. I was on my second whisky and very pleased to see him.

The Association for Educational and Training Technology was the main professional organisation for educational technologists at the time. It produced an academic journal and a yearbook, and organised an annual international conference (ETIC) with published proceedings. I joined the board of the association and was usually involved in the conferences, giving a paper, running a workshop, producing an exhibition or chairing a session. In 1976, Dundee College of Education hosted ETIC and I was part of the planning group. At the conference dinner in 1975 in London, we had given every delegate a miniature bottle of whisky with a sticker advertising our conference. We had several generous sponsors including Stewarts Whisky distillers, whose famous "Cream of the Barley" was produced in Dundee. They gave us a thousand miniatures and several litre bottles of a single malt. Another local firm produced tartan purses and comb holders for all 450 delegates.

Dundee College of Education insisted that female students going into school on placement did not wear trousers and, if they did, they were sent home. Lecturers were meant to dress in a smart and sober way. One day in about 1978 I wore a black skirt, pink blouse and pink tights the same shade as the blouse (it was the height of fashion!). At coffee time the Dean of Women announced publicly that she thought my tights were inappropriate wear. However, she did not forbid my wardrobe, so the next day I wore bright blue tights which again coordinated with my outfit. I was delighted that half a dozen of my female colleagues also wore brightly-coloured tights!

There was a bank of bright red metal mailboxes outside the staff dining room, and we each had a named box. At the start of each academic year a pack of white chalk would appear in every box. I did not use chalk often, preferring the overhead projector, flipchart or audio-visual materials. But by then my friend David was teaching in a poorly-resourced community centre in the Midlands. We usually met up a couple of times a year when we went south to visit our parents, so I passed my chalks on to him. One year we found a condom in each mailbox. I think it was to do with sex education in schools, and the college was primarily about teacher education. Some of the single female lecturers were most upset. I remember another case of righteous indignation when a lecturer was stopped for speeding. She was late for a meeting and did not know where it was (before the days of satnavs). The police breathalysed her, and she was furious as she was teetotal and would not even eat a liqueur chocolate. After she had complied, she rounded on the officers and said they had now made her even later and she still did not know where to go. So she received a police escort to her meeting.

I remember going to a demonstration of a word processor in the secretarial pool. This would allow the typists to store frequently-used paragraphs for future use without having to type everything from scratch. In those days, all official correspondence was meant to be typed in the office. The lecturer would receive a carbon copy, and a second copy was held in a central file. I was told that on Saturday mornings the Principal would read through all the letters to keep abreast of all aspects of the college business.

DipEdTech

My new job was to develop and teach a postgraduate diploma in educational technology (DipEdTech). It was a one-year full-time programme for teachers and trainers. The first year had a small intake of eleven Scottish and international students. We had three Egyptian medics, a trainer from Iran and one from Venezuela, two FE lecturers from Scotland, one lecturer from our own college, one from the art college, and two school-teachers. One of the Egyptian doctors said as soon as he arrived that he was looking for a Scottish wife. And he found one. At the end of the academic year he married his landlady's daughter, took her home to Egypt, and they had three children.

The course was very practical and also included a few educational visits. One student worked at a teachers' resource centre in Fife, which we visited. The centre had access to a glider, and he arranged for any student who wished to have a short trip over the Fife countryside. José from Venezuela was always keen for any experience and signed up before he had managed to find out what a glider was. But he did appreciate the trip.

Over the next few years most students were teachers, lecturers or trainers from the UK, but we had a few from overseas including Iran, Chile and Sudan. We had a "Catch-22" situation with one international student. His employer would only guarantee the fees once he had a firm offer of a place on the course, and the college would not offer a place until the fees were guaranteed. I explained the dilemma to a senior manager who wrote a letter on headed paper offering a place. This did the trick, the fees were paid and the student arrived, even though that particular person had no right to make a formal offer.

One Sudanese student brought his wife and three young children with him, and none of them could speak English. Kadok kept missing classes to take his children to the dentist, and I asked one of our social work lecturers if she could help. She arranged a support worker for the family and also discovered that the children were suffering from the cold. We sent out a message round the college staff and people donated lots of warm clothes for the kids and some toys. We took them round one evening. Kadok and his wife made us welcome and gave us coffee and some traditional biscuits. Then we opened the bags and gradually removed the clothes, and the children excitedly decided who would wear what. When we reached the toys, it became a real party.

Once the Shah was deposed in 1979, we lost our source of students from Iran. We did receive some mail from ex-students with postage stamps bearing gory pictures of dripping blood. The post stopped, and a few months later I was amazed to get a phone call from one of the young female students. Fatemeh had been recruited into the army but had been shot in the shoulder and was recovering in hospital in Tehran.

My ideas did not always fit with those of the college. I designed the timetable, allow-

DipEdTech, first cohort. I am in the middle, holding their mascot.

ing one and a half days per week that were unallocated so students could work independently on their assignments and projects. The vice principal felt this would encourage laziness and that their study time should be tightly regulated. My plan was vindicated when the students worked very hard and achieved excellent results. My students were highly motivated and wanted to do well, and they managed their own learning effectively. A rigid timetable may not achieve anything other than a full attendance register. Students may be physically present but may be thinking about something else or, nowadays, even interacting with online social media.

Then there was the problem with norm-referenced assessment. Assessments in the college were graded on a scale from zero (fail) to seven (excellent). Most students were expected to fall into the middle area, and their grades were stretched to cover the extremes. It was all about comparison between students rather than the quality of their achievements. So if an average student had a lot of bright classmates, they would get a low grade. The same student with some less clever peers would get a higher grade. This approach seemed unfair and unhelpful, and I preferred the criterion-referenced system. We specified the assessment criteria linked to the learning outcomes, and if the students met the criteria then they succeeded. So any number of students could pass or fail. To get round the 0-7 grading scale I decided to give everyone who passed a seven, and those who did not got a zero. Eventually I was allowed to grade my student as pass or fail or distinction for very high-quality work.

The course covered the basics of the EdTech approach, setting precise objectives, designing appropriate learning activities, assessing achievements and evaluating the whole process. The students planned courses, designed assessment methods and created learning materials in various media. They were supported by a wide range of technical staff such as photographers, graphics artists, printers, and a complete film production crew. Each cohort made a short film as a group project. In one case I was an extra and had to lie down on the ground in front of a moving car. Even though I trusted the driver and the car was moving slowly, I was very relieved when the shooting of that scene was over. I wanted the learning to be as useful as possible so students had to create a range of audiovisual resources in their own subject area. They also had to complete an implementation project, usually trying out some of their materials in a real situation and evaluating the pilot. The Scottish students did a project within their own institution, and the doctors did projects at the medical school through links with Ronnie Harden. For other overseas students, I negotiated opportunities in local schools and colleges for them to try out their resources.

After a couple of years it became obvious that the market for a full-time course was decreasing. British teachers and lecturers could not be seconded for so long, and international funding became harder. The answer was distance learning. Students could stay in post, which meant that their projects were more authentic. The teaching was old technology – by interactive booklets, audio tapes and film-strips delivered by

DipEdTech Cohort 2, shown shooting a film.

post. Fortunately the staff were already used to designing self-study materials, and the college was equipped to produce multiple copies. We packaged the course into chunks of content; this was before modularisation insisted that all bits of knowledge deserved the same amount of time and effort.

There were eighty students, but the secretary in charge of the stationery cupboard complained when I requested a hundred large envelopes to send out the course materials. The college sold the learning units to other colleges and universities and gave the royalties to the authors. The college library did lend some books to students, delivered and returned by post. Most students did not have easy access to an educational library, and the internet and electronic books were still in the future. We managed to negotiate with several publishers to allow us to reprint chapters from their books. These were posted to the students, but they had to be returned and re-used.

The learning packages were complemented by residential on-campus weeks, and by tutorial support by phone and post. Most students worked during the day, so the tutors gave them their home phone numbers. This was rarely abused, although I did get one phone call on Christmas Day from someone of a different religion. I also remember a call late at night from a student who said he had read the same page five times and still could not understand it. I realised this was not the time for a tutorial about the content, so I advised him to stop work and have a whisky, knowing that was his favourite tipple. We used 3-part NCR (no carbon required) paper to give formative and summative feedback. The top copy was posted to the student, the second copy was for the tutor, and the third copy went into the student's file kept by the administrator.

The on-campus blocks were popular and an important part of the course, allowing students to engage in interactive workshops and group work and to develop peer support partnerships. We put them into groups to design a short educational input to be presented to the whole group on the last day. They were creative and innovative as well as informative. I remember one presentation about body language which used the audience to illustrate several important points. They asked us to put our left hand on our waist and hold the right arm out. We followed the instructions and were told to lean to the right while singing "I'm a little teapot short and stout, tip me over and pour me out". When we stopped laughing they explained that although most of the presentation was authentic, they had also made a bet to get me to sing a nursery rhyme.

We knew that distance learning could be isolating, so we made deliberate efforts to support students on an individual basis. Each student had a personal tutor who provided encouragement and advice as well as detailed formative help with assignments. At the start we sent out photographs of all the tutors together with welcome messages on audiocassettes. I had learned from doing some work with Radio Tay that you can hear the warmth of a smile, so we smiled as we recorded out introductions in a soundproof booth. We maintained contact with our students by letter, phone, visit and latterly by email. Pen pals have built up relationships for years, and some tutor student links flourished too. I still exchange Christmas cards with some of my students from the 1980s, and I still meet a couple regularly even though they live miles away. I have always treated my students more like colleagues and respected the vast knowledge they have in their particular area.

I remember one student who told me during a college block that his new baby had a rare genetic condition and would not live long. A few months later he emailed me to say she had died. I sent a sympathy card and, at his request, informed the rest of the students via our newsletter. It made me think about forms of communication and which were appropriate. He emailed because it would be quicker than writing a letter and easier to correct. I did not think a reply email would seem compassionate enough and felt that a carefully chosen card, handwritten and posted, showed my sympathy better.

One of my students was a teacher at the Royal Blind School in Edinburgh and I visited him there to discuss his project. I watched Derek teach a science lesson which was full of clever devices to support visually impaired pupils. An audio thermometer could be set to a required level using a Braille scale and, when it reached that heat, it bleeped. Ironically, they were studying the eye on the day I visited. First they traced the shape of the eye using 3D polystyrene cut-outs, then they handled some cows' eyes that Derek had obtained from a local abattoir. It was bizarre to see blind children touching the slimy eyeballs and eventually holding a lens in their hand.

We wanted to encourage computer-based learning, so with a government grant we purchased 30 BBC computers in suitcases and a range of learning packages. Each computer was delivered to a student to examine and critique for six weeks before they sent it on to the next student on the list using a prepaid collect and deliver service. Back then it was impossible to imagine the online systems we have now.

We developed a partnership with the International Training College in Enschede in the Netherlands, which trained pilots and aerial photographers. I went over to carry out a short induction to the course and to meet the students. It was a fascinating place, now part of the University of Twente. They showed me the equipment they used to make aerial photos, looking for everything from crop devastation by locusts to freshwater springs within the oceans. They also put me in a simulator plane and turned up the turbulence so it made it almost impossible to control, but it was an interesting experience.

While I was in the country I also held a preliminary meeting with training officers from Shell. They were keen to investigate distance learning for their offshore workers and wanted to engage us as consultants. They really wanted a couple of people to work with them full-time, so I explained we did not have the staffing capacity, no matter how much they paid.

My flight back was cancelled due to a firemen's strike at Edinburgh Airport. I was so impressed with the staff at Schiphol Airport, who offered to transfer my flight to Aberdeen or Glasgow or Newcastle. They then told me the times of trains from each UK city to Dundee so I could make an informed choice. I flew to Glasgow and arrived in Dundee only a couple of hours late.

Another useful partnership was with the Portuguese Navy, and we had quite a few trainers from there over several years. They usually arrived at the college blocks with bottles of port and often small gifts from faraway places. I have a beautiful pink quartz stone rose from an African desert, a porcelain dish emblazoned with the crest of the Portuguese Navy, and a leather presentation case containing a model of a mariner's astrolabe from the Museu de Marinha with a metal tag "Portuguese Navy. Ed Tech Probation. Scotland. 19-30 May 97".

The tutors held a debriefing meeting at the end of each block, and it became a tradition that we sipped the port wine then. The students were required to meet deadlines and maintain regular contact, but we had to allow exceptions for those working in submarines on extended manoeuvres with radio silence.

The motto of the college was "Disco ut Doceum": "I learn in order that I may teach". In prac-

A striking gift from the Portuguese Navy

tice I felt it worked better the other way round: "I teach in order that I may learn". I certainly always learned a great deal from my students, especially those from other countries and different cultures.

Like most academics, I did my share of external examining. It is an arduous, poorly paid experience but a measure of *quid pro quo* is necessary for the system to operate. The pool of academics who could appropriately examine my DipEdTech was fairly small. We all knew each other, and met regularly at conferences and other events. The external examiner would read a sample of scripts before the exam board. They usually met with students and tutors, as well as being involved in the formal part of the meeting which looked at student progress. They normally arrived the night before, and some of the tutors took them out to dinner. On one occasion I said goodbye as I planned to go to my local pub quiz at nine o'clock. The external asked if she could come too, as she was a keen quizzer. So she joined our team (we came second) and I drove her back to her hotel. We chatted about the quiz the next day while we were waiting to start the meeting, and the chairperson said that such fraternising was inappropriate. How was it any different from a dinner paid for by the college?

About fifteen other institutions in the UK offered a qualification in EdTech and CET arranged regular conferences for us to share ideas and debate key issues. These were lively and productive events, but sometimes the discussions became heated. There was some tension between those who focused on the media and those who focused on the learning. The technology aspect of EdTech was really about a systems approach, not about gadgets. Another area of disagreement was whether the qualification was at undergraduate or postgraduate level. Our course was clearly at postgrad level; our students were already graduates and were applying ideas in their own context. The work in their assignments was both academic and professional. Some years later the Scottish Credit and Qualifications Framework made it easier to justify the level of a course, and you could match the learning outcomes and assessments to a specific set of benchmarks. The SCQF was a useful guide in designing programmes, but sometimes it led to a box-ticking mentality.

The college became well known for its approach to individualised learning, and all courses were expected to have a quarter of the time in this mode. The materials used various media: printed booklets, audio tape, slides, filmstrips and video. They all had an aligned curriculum design with stated learning objectives, clear interactive structure and self-tests. They were produced to a high standard by our printing and audio-visual staff. The prime audience was the college's own students, but the learning materials were sold to other colleges and universities and the authors received royalty payments. Not all staff were entirely happy with this move to individualised learning, feeling that it was simply to justify the expense of the learning resource centre. I was asked to act as a consultant, helping my colleagues develop materials, and I enjoyed this role. It led to involvement in many in-service courses and in the design of learning packages as part of national initiatives. I regarded myself as a generic trainer.

Colleges of education and polytechnics did not have university status to award their own qualifications. The institutions and the courses needed to be approved by the Council for National Academic Awards. I was involved in getting my own course validated, as well as sitting on panels for other courses and institutions. Most meetings were held in the London offices of CNAA. They provided lunch – always sandwiches and always black forest gateau that was never fully defrosted. It is still my least-favourite dessert.

Resource-based learning was becoming increasingly popular, and CNAA set up a small working party of ten academics to visit a range of institutions. I was honoured to be part of it. We split into small groups and interviewed staff and students, examined learning resources and analysed systems. We produced a case study of each visit. After several months we met for three days to write our report and come up with some guidelines "to provide an aide-memoire on the kinds of questions which may be raised when validating courses which are learning resource-based." We stressed the importance of staff training and of student support, and I am pleased we included comments about how much time was needed for an effective system. I was the only female member and the only one from Scotland, and someone called me a "twofer". This tokenistic comment meant that I hit two categories, so I was worth "two for one". I was furious, as I knew I had made a valuable contribution to the project and was there on merit. I have a female mixed-race colleague who walks with two sticks; she would be a real bonus!

We were accommodated in the Grand Brighton Hotel, later bombed during a Conservative Party conference. We worked hard, but managed a few bracing walks on the beach. This was 1976 and the nation was gripped by a TV drama, *A Bouquet of Barbed Wire*, starring Frank Finlay and Susan Penhaligon. The final episode was shown one night while we were away and everyone retired to their bedroom to watch, meeting in the hotel bar afterwards. This was before the days of streaming and box sets. If you missed a programme, you missed it. The only alternative was to ask someone at home to tape it on their VHS (or Betamax!) video recorder.

Three organisations – CNAA, CET, and SCET – occupied vast premises, employed many staff and had a major impact on education from the 1960s. But by the turn of the century they had all been dissolved and now warrant just a few lines in Wikipedia. Higher education institutions merged with universities, or became universities and were able to award their own degrees. Validation and approval decisions were undertaken by SHEFC (the Scottish Higher and Further Education Funding Council; now the Scottish Funding Council). The use of technology in teaching and flexible delivery methods became mainstream. Professional bodies began to play a much larger part in curriculum design and approval.

Quality assurance has become significant. Universities have internal systems for the validation and regular review of courses, but still need to satisfy external stakeholders. Such events are a bit like an OFSTED inspection. We became adept at writing programme documentation in "validationese", using the language required by SCQF and professional bodies. I usually spent the first part of teaching on a new module discussing the learning outcomes and assessment requirements with the students and getting them to put them into words they understood. In my career I have needed external approval for my courses and projects from the City and Guilds, CNAA, the General Teaching Council for Scotland, SHEFC, the Higher Education Academy and the Quality Assurance Agency. In every case I have also become involved with the organisation, helping to develop programmes in other institutions. This shift from poacher to gamekeeper allowed me to understand their (sometimes strange) criteria and to enhance my own critical abilities.

South-East Asia

My trips to Malaysia and Thailand were the most exotic in my academic travels. I worked on several projects with Professor Lewis Elton from the University of Surrey (and father of Ben Elton, comedian and author). We provided a range of staff development experiences for lecturers at the Universiti Sains Malaysia (USM) in Penang. We were funded by the Inter-University Council for Higher Education, and were invited for several purposes:

- To run some educational workshops and seminars for university academics.
- To provide initial training in teaching and learning methods for new lecturers.

- To explore strategies for ongoing staff training and for working with a very varied student population.

We also visited a number of other educational establishments in the region in order to develop a general model of staff development, which led to several publications. "We will concentrate on the teaching aspect of staff development and our main aim is to bring lecturers to develop the same professional attitude to their teaching as to their research. If a lecturer is more knowledgeable and better skilled in their teaching, then the institution should benefit in terms of results, and the lecturer in terms of job satisfaction."

We visited for six weeks in the summer of 1978 and ran a series of workshops and planning meetings. A university in a developing country has to meet the current needs of the population, the traditions of the country, and the international academic standards. We used a problem-solving approach with senior managers to develop a training strategy. Our eventual aim was to establish staff development programmes based on local resources and support for several institutions in South East Asia. The main intention of a staff developer or a consultant should be to make themselves redundant as they have guided their clients to self-sufficiency.

Our flight out was on a Singapore Airlines jumbo jet. It was luxurious. The food was delicious, although I was daunted when I realised how many cows had been slaughtered to provide fillet steaks for that many people. Several times we were brought fresh moist flannels and they were sometimes warm, sometimes hot and sometimes ice cold. But the temperature was always just what you wanted. At one stopover we were joined by a choir of Chinese schoolchildren and their teachers who had been performing at an international music festival. My heart sank as I anticipated noisy disruptions. But they behaved perfectly. As we taxied into Singapore they stood up (health and safety regulations ignored) and sang. It was beautiful, and much appreciated by all the passengers who gave them a round of applause. As we left the aircraft, we were each given a garland of flowers by the stewardess.

Penang is a small island a few miles off the West coast of Malaysia, now connected by a bridge. Back then we had to cross by ferry. I visited the toilet on board and was dismayed that the toilet bowl was simply an open hole to the sea below. When the water became choppy it was a bit like using a very cold bidet – not recommended. George Town is a thriving city, with roads full of cars, cycles, motorbikes and trishaws (cycle rickshaws) all vying for space. Yet a few miles away you are in rural villages with small thatched huts on stilts and free-roaming goats.

In Penang we were in a guesthouse in what had been the governor's house on the university campus. There was constant background noise, from the insects outside and from the aircon inside, although that did break down frequently. We attended the university's sports day and I was amused that it started with a parade of bagpipers wearing kilts and playing Scottish tunes. We were invited to a dinner party and served an array of dishes including a well-known delicacy of "hundred-year eggs". Actually they were only three months old, but had been buried and turned black. My favourite refreshment in the town was coconut milk. The coconuts were stored in an enormous fridge. The café owner would chop the top off with a machete and give you a straw for the milk and a spoon to scrape out the soft flesh. The majority of the hard coconut was discarded.

Most of the academic staff were Chinese with a few Indian and a few Malay. The Malays were the indigenous population, the "bumiputra" or "sons of the soil". They were the most numerous race in the country and controlled the government,

Our guest house; formerly the governor's house

but they were less well educated and less wealthy than the Chinese. They introduced laws to try to ensure equality. So Chinese shop owners were told to employ a percentage of Malay workers or face a fine. Many chose to pay the fine. You cannot change attitudes by legislation.

Our workshops were based on old technology. We used overhead projector transparencies, audio tapes, slides,

Cooking dinner at the guest house.

Graffiti on the USM Campus

videotapes and printed handouts. We also developed ideas on flipcharts using coloured markers. We travelled with our training materials, but we had been warned not to bring any Blu-Tack as a colleague had been stopped by airport security thinking it was plastic explosive.

We ran a course for new lecturers and trained up two local staff development officers to run it in the future. The new trainers had briefing and debriefing sessions with us in which we explained our ra-

Dinner with USM staff. I am wearing a batik dress. Lewis Elton is on my right.

tionale for the course and discussed key issues. One of the first things we did was to explain our own personal philosophy of teaching and learning. This was not to try to impose our views but to explain our values. We then invited them to think about their own philosophy. Some were surprised to realise that they already had a distinct philosophy but they had not articulated it before. For some it brought up tensions between their beliefs and the expectations of the university.

The course lasted for five days and was held on the beautiful island resort of Langkawi, the Jewel of Kedah. This is about sixty miles north-west of Penang, and we travelled by bus and ferry. It happened to be during Ramadan, and the participants who were Muslims abstained from lunch while we enjoyed a feast. I was concerned to notice that one lecturer who was several months pregnant, and thus had a medical reason not to fast, still chose to spend the lunch hour with her colleagues and was not eating. While I respected her decision, I found it sad that subtle peer pressure and cultural norms were perhaps damaging her unborn child. I realise that some people would consider my thoughts insensitive or inappropriate, but that is what I felt at the time.

The course covered a range of topics including learning objectives, small group teaching, lecturing to large groups, assessment methods, audio-visual communication and evaluation, all introduced as interactive workshops. We also gave every participant the

Langkawi resort.

opportunity to deliver a short piece of teaching, which was then analysed by self-reflection, peer comments and tutor critique. The course was quite intensive and the participants really gained in knowledge, ideas and confidence. They gave us each a beautiful batik picture as a memento. I still have mine hanging on my wall. At the end of our visit we also received a formal gift of an engraved plaque from the vice chancellor. It is in a wooden box emblazoned with the university crest and is inscribed as shown in the image below.

It was fascinating to compare our ideas with a different culture, but it was hard work. We had come with several workshops already prepared, but new needs emerged so we often worked late at night creating activities for the following day. One area in particular was formative assessment. The pervading view was that assessment was for certification, rather than for learning. We ran some activities to demonstrate

A treasured memento of my time in Malaysia.

different ways to provide support and feedback for the learners during a course rather than at the end. We discussed the
value of self and peer assessment and shared examples from
our own courses in the UK.

We were allowed a couple of weekends off and visited
the Cameron Highlands, where it was cool enough to grow
strawberries. We went to Kota Bharu on the East coast and
walked on what used to be called "The Beach of Passionate
Love". In keeping with Islamic sensibilities, it is now called
"Moonlight Beach". My only emotion there was a negative
one, as a coconut fell from a tree and bruised my shoulder.

One of the British expats who was a lecturer at USM
came to see us with a dilemma. He had a mixed class of well-
educated Chinese and poorly-educated Malay students, and
had been told that the same percentage of each race had to
pass his course. He had to drop his assessment standards or
risk losing his job. The university authorities wanted their
local population to be well qualified, but providing meaning-
less degrees was not the answer. It seemed clear to me that
they needed to introduce an access course after school and
before university which could bring the students up to an appropriate entry standard.

Here is a short account I wrote after my first visit to
Penang in 1978:

I walk slowly past the bakery, but there are several customers so I get some fruit from the shop next
door first. The tiny Malaysian bananas, no more
than three inches long, are so full of flavour. I love
the Penang curries, sweet and mild with succulent
fruit and coconut milk, but not for every meal. So I

have eggs for breakfast, and bread, cheese and fruit for lunch.

There are still people in the bakers but I cannot wait any longer so I sidle in, looking at my feet. But to no avail. The baker sees me, beams, and hurries the person he is serving out the door. Ignoring the other customers he comes over to me to see what I want. I ask for a white loaf, pointing to the pile on the counter. But he walks into the back dusting off his floury hands on his grimy trousers and returns with a new loaf. It is still warm and smells delicious. While he wraps it and takes the money, I see his wife waving from the back workroom. She wipes her warm brow and continues to knead the dough. I remind myself that the oven heat will sterilise the bread.

I smile apologetically to the other customers. I do not ask him to treat me like a VIP. I do not want this "old colonial" preferential treatment. I feel uncomfortable but if I complain the baker will be hurt. So I try to call when the shop is empty.

I take my purchases and walk back to the car. I jump over the storm drain, remembering the deluge last week. The local men stood at the gaps in the drains clubbing the rats to death as they were swept along by the monsoon rains. The excited frenzy became more than just an exercise in pest control as they vied with each other to kill the greatest number. Add red coats and bugle calls and another colonial tradition would be maintained.

Back on campus, I have my simple lunch with the tasty, nutty bread. I am here for the summer, running courses for the university lecturers. I live in the guesthouse for visiting consultants. We each have our own small chalet of bedroom, lounge, kitchen and bathroom and there is a central house where we eat dinner together. It is served in elegant surroundings using quality china and napery, yet it is prepared on an open fire in the backyard in an enormous wok three feet across.

I take my second shower of the day even though it is only early afternoon. The climate is not too hot, about thirty degrees, but the humidity is one hundred percent and the atmosphere is totally enervating. The ceiling fans merely move the warm damp air around the room yet they create a cool illusion.

Two small lizards dart along the lounge wall, playing hide and seek behind the picture frames. There is an ant highway through my chalet. They come in through a grating beside the front door go across the floor and out through a gap in the kitchen wall. I cannot get rid of them so I just step over them. They never deviate from their highway by more than a couple of inches. When they reach the fridge a few bold ants crawl along the flex and up inside the appliance. They do not get far before the temperature makes them torpid. Every evening I scrape a handful of comatose ants off the salad shelf in my fridge. I drop them onto their highway where they quickly warm up and scuttle away. My definition of the tropics is where the wildlife cannot distinguish between indoors and outdoors.

We visited Kuala Lumpur too, which is a thriving metropolis, and gave staff development workshops on curriculum design, assessment and evaluation. The lecturers were very interested in our approach to individualised learning as a way to reach more rural students, and we discussed ways of offering continued training and support. I was intrigued to see a notice saying "No Durians" in hotels and at the airport. Was this an example of racial discrimination, or were durians animals? But no, durians are fruits which some people find delicious to eat. But they have a disgusting overpowering smell that lingers for days after they have been removed.

We travelled to Thailand to run several educational workshops for lecturers and to hold seminars with senior staff. The Chulalongkorn University in Bangkok gave mass lectures to over a thousand students, most of whom could only see and hear the lecturer on closed circuit TV. Some of the staff wanted our opinion on their learning packages, but this was difficult as the Thai language uses a totally different script; for example, the word for "education" is การศึกษา. We explained our design principles and hoped they would be able to transfer them.

We were accommodated in a luxury hotel which gave us a complementary basket of exotic local fruit. I sampled them all, and most were delicious. But one was so sticky it stuck my lips together. I scrubbed them with a soapy flannel and, although my lips recovered, the flannel did not. After several washes it was still glutinous and I had to throw it away. We visited one of the floating markets and the famous Wat Phra Kaew (the Temple of the Emerald Buddha), and added some gold leaf to the walls. One evening we were taken out to dinner and there was a spectacular floor show. This included shadow puppets and the elegant Thai dancers with amazingly flexible fingers.

The senior academic who hosted us was married to a policeman, and he told us fascinating stories about the local crime rate. He said that assassinations were quite common and you could hire a "hit man" for the equivalent of about two pounds, or double for an important target. Some friends in Penang had asked us to bring back some Thai whisky, so we asked where we could purchase some. The policeman came back the next day with a bottle of whisky that he had confiscated from a criminal.

While in Penang we identified two important issues for USM: the wide range of ability in the students, and a substantial programme of correspondence courses. These suggested that individualised learning might be a useful way forward, allowing students to work at their own pace. Back in the UK we designed self-study materials and enrolled some senior staff on a distance learning course. We exchanged activities, formative assessment and tutorial support by mail in early 1979.

When we returned in the summer of 1979, we had follow-up discussions with these participants. We ran more workshops for lecturers on aspects of teaching and learning in HE. In some of these we were assisted by the staff development officers from the Langkawi workshop. We were pleased to note that individualised learning materials had been introduced into some courses. These followed the format we had suggested: clear learning objectives, attractively presented content and frequent self-tests to measure progress. Some were little more than study guides linked to a standard textbook, but they all allowed students to learn at their own rate.

This helped to reduce the inequality of educational backgrounds a little. A new Teaching-Learning Advisory Unit had been established to provide training and support for academics.

After our second visit to Penang we established some ongoing courses at Dundee and Surrey which led to a couple of joint papers. We developed relationships with several HE institutions in South East Asia. Some members of staff from USM joined my DipEdTech course in Dundee; several joined a specially-designed programme in Surrey lasting three months, and others enrolled for a distance learning certificate. They were introduced to the practical implementation of curriculum design and in all cases their assignments were structured to be applied to their own context. These collaborations were fruitful for several years. However, there was one problem case. One of the visitors took our printed self-study packages back home and changed the front cover so they looked like his own work. This was discovered by accident when a colleague visited the following year and recognised our materials. Malaysia was not a signatory of the international copyright agreements, and it would have been hard to challenge it in law. However, a quiet word from vice principal to vice principal across the international world of academia resulted in them buying some materials from us with the correct covers.

The festival of the hungry ghosts happened during our second visit. This is a Chinese celebration and included street parades with brightly coloured floats. A few days later there was a Hindu festival with music and firewalking. We were painted with a small tilaka mark on our forehead as a form of greeting. My memories are of friendly people, impressive tem-

ples, delicious street food, beautiful batik clothes and groups
of inquisitive monkeys in the trees.

Australia

I had never had any particular wish to go to the Antipodes,
but an unexpected invite sounded like an interesting challenge.
I knew Dave Boud in Glasgow in the early 1970s, long before
he moved to Australia and became an internationally re-
nowned expert on assessment in HE. We met regularly at conferences and meetings, and in 1979 he phoned me up to ask if I
would like to do staff development work in Australia for a
year. I talked to the college about a leave of absence, but they
would only let me go for six months. Murdoch University
wanted someone to act as an educational consultant on a variety of projects and in the end they agreed to appoint me together with another person at the same time. This was not a
sabbatical. I was employed by Murdoch University in Perth
in Western Australia, and I paid Australian taxes. Dundee
agreed to continue to pay my superannuation and national
insurance contributions, and they employed someone on a
short-term contract to carry out my teaching. This person was
paid at lower grade, so they did not lose any money.

The trip occurred immediately after my second visit to
Penang, so I just kept flying south. This meant that when I
left Dundee I had to take everything I needed for Malaysia
and Australia. When I landed in Perth in the early hours of
the morning I was exhausted after an intensive time in Malaysia and a long flight. We were asked to remain in our seats
as two officials entered the plane and sprayed insecticides over

us. What a different welcome from the fragrant flowers in Singapore!

In Australia, we two British educational technologists shared a house we rented from a lecturer who was on sabbatical. I paid extra to use his car. We both worked in the Educational Services and Teaching Resources department (ESTR), and it was handy to discuss projects at home. ESTR ran staff development workshops and provided individual consultancy for staff across the university. Many Australian universities had similar staff development units, and their members had considerable problems with status and academic acceptance, even though they were well qualified. Even in Dundee, staff in the Academic Skills Centre were on an "academic-related" pay scale, different from the academic scale for lecturing staff.

Murdoch used acronyms for many of its courses. Thus Mathematical and Statistical Bases of Inquiry became MSBSI or "Mizzy-bizzy", and Functional and Plant Anatomy became FAPA or "Fapper". These strange names were bad enough for courses, but they were also used to identify the course leaders who became known as Dr Mizzy-bizzy and Mr Fapper!

I worked as an educational consultant on several projects across the university including evaluation, course design and producing videos and tape-slide programmes. I was asked by the personnel department to create a resource to help graduating students get jobs by improving their skills at writing applications and responding at interviews. I worked with the personnel manager, Ted, and he and his wife Judy became friends. A couple of years later they responded to the invitation I offered liberally in Australia to come and stay if they were ever in Scotland. Quite a few people took up the invite, usually with short notice. So Ted phoned me up one day and said that he and Judy would be in Scotland the following weekend. I invited them to stay for a couple of days on their tour "to cover the whole of the country" within a week. Andy and I had already booked tickets for a play and were able to get another two seats. It was a strange farce and any characters who misbehaved were threatened with deportation to Western Australia. This destination was a chance occurrence, but Ted and Judy were convinced we had persuaded the theatre to change Siberia for Western Australia in their honour.

The resource I developed with Ted was called "Job-hunt", and was a video plus workbook. The workbook contained detailed analyses of applications and interviews and lots of practical tasks to develop the participants' skills. The video followed the fate of three candidates. I wrote outline scripts and students from the drama department improvised. I had scripted films and videos in Glasgow and Dundee, working with professional production units. But here I had the chance to be director and video editor too. I got quite a thrill out of saying "Quiet. Run camera. Action!"

The professor at the vet school asked me to video his seminars and then discuss how he could improve them. He was concerned about the low level of involvement from the students. He knew they were capable but they seemed very reluctant to speak up in class. In the session I recorded, each student in turn presented a problem case and then the class had to solve it as a group. The student presentations were clear and concise, but every time they posed a problem, the professor jumped in with the answer. He did not give the students a chance to think about it and they seemed to be intimidated by his presence. He was very enthusiastic and simply wanted to share his vast knowledge and experience, but it actually inhibited the learning. When we reviewed the video together after the class, he was mortified to see how he had dominated the proceedings. Future sessions were handled by a more junior member of staff, who was instructed not to comment until the students had spent some time discussing the problem.

The staff in the university library asked for my help in explaining the rules and classification system to new students. We devised an audio-visual self-study programme which the students loved. The staff had more time to deal with specific queries. I followed the basic design principles we used in Dundee – state objectives, design mastery tests, create structured sequences using a variety of examples to suit a varied audience, build in quizzes and make an attractive colourful package. In thanks they gave me a beautiful Australian cookbook which I have used many times, even though some ingredients are not available in Scotland.

The Scottish Education Department had given me a small fee to produce a report about distance learning in Australia. I visited seven universities and colleges and talked to staff. I interviewed several students, and I remember one in particular. She lived on a remote farm and had received high grades for every module in her first two years of study, but her performance had plummeted in the last six months. Sometimes this can happen as a student progresses to a higher level within a degree, but the tutors thought she was very able and were concerned about her. I went out to visit her and interview her about her studies. She was pragmatic and honest. She made me a cup of tea then went into another room and came back holding a very small baby. She was so committed to her course that she had taken an exam in hospital just five days after giving birth. She explained that she now had a new priority that took a lot of time and energy. She knew just how hard she needed to work to get a pass grade and that was all she needed. She was strategic learner and I had to applaud her logic.

The students were not regarded as distance learners but as external students. They felt like, and seemed to be treated as, less important than the fulltime internal students. The biggest problem seemed to be the lack of support and a sense of isolation. There was often a long delay in providing feedback because tutors did not give the work priority, and the mail system was inadequate in rural areas with only two deliveries a week. Attempts to form local self-help groups were not successful because the students were too thinly spread. Things are so different now with advances in technology, but there are still problems with internet connectivity. The external students liked audio tapes recorded just for them as they gave the course a human touch. They were so popular that some admitted to making copies before they returned them.

The conclusions of my report discussed the importance of help in study skills, the need for relevant quality learning materials and the requirement for efficient admin procedures. I felt that many issues were relevant to Scotland. This is my final paragraph:

It seems appropriate to increase the number and variety of distance learning courses in Scotland. This mode of learning can serve many groups in the community, from adult learners to apprentices. My overall feeling is one of optimism, since I believe that this approach, especially if planned in a flexible way, can fill several educational gaps in Scotland now.

I was also invited to run staff development workshops in Canberra, Melbourne and Sydney, so I travelled across several time zones. In Sydney I marvelled at the iconic bridge, walked on Bondi Beach, and listened to a concert sitting on the steps outside the opera house. I took a plane from Sydney to Newcastle to visit a colleague in the medical school there. It was a short trip of about 100 miles along the east coast and the plane was very small. We ran into a spectacular thunderstorm and could see the lighting jumping between clouds and hitting the ground and starting bush fires. I stayed with friends in Canberra and realised just how many previous colleagues I had in Australia. It was great to catch up with them.

I always try to reflect on my experiences and identify any general learning that can apply to future situations. Together with the director of ESTR I wrote a short article about the role of visiting staff. It was called "The Other Side of the Fence", and John Cowan (the director of the Open University in Scotland) penned a reply which was published with it. The debate focused on the need for clear expectations by all parties, and we agreed on certain guidelines. One senior person in the host institution needs to take responsibility to introduce the visitor to key people and to explain the systems and nuances of the organisation. It helps to involve the visitor in a "quick win", such as running a seminar or joining a very short-term project. The visitor needs to provide a record of what they do and to ensure clear mechanisms for continuing any work not completed by the time they leave. Domestic arrangements must be sorted out quickly. It is important that all parties benefit from the experience.

I was impressed by the work ethic and the egalitarian society in Australia. I was offered several opportunities to extend my stay and work in other institutions. I was fascinated by the flora and fauna since it was biologically so different from anything I had experienced before. Food was very cheap, cultural events were vibrant, but there was no real sense of history. I enjoyed the beautiful and strange Australian flowers, the blue skies which have a depth of colour never seen in Britain, and the "Fremantle Doctor" – the pleasant cool breeze which comes in from the sea. My final memory of Australia was being taken to hear a beautiful rendition of Handel's *Messiah* en-route to my midnight flight home just before Christmas 1979.

Open Learning

The DipEdTech by distance learning ran successfully for many years, and my colleagues and I developed our expertise in the discipline of open learning. The training of secondary teachers in Dundee declined and was eventually removed, and several staff from other disciplines moved into what was now the open learning and academic studies department (OLAS). Staff from science, home economics, religious education, physical education and technical education took the DipEdTech qualification and then became course tutors. We offered a certificate course in open learning, using open learning both as a topic and a delivery mechanism. We also acted as consultants in the design of open and distance programmes and worked with the Department of Health and Social Services and the Manpower Services Commission. On one occasion the MSC invited me to attend a meeting with business leaders to discuss training options using open learning. I was the only female and the youngest person in the board room. I was there as an expert consultant but everyone assumed I was a minute secretary until my role was explained. Many places now used an open learning approach for their in-house training. It was clear that open learning gave students much more control over their own learning, not just in where and when to study. This autonomy empowered students, building their confidence. This was decades before the idea of co-creating curricula with students became popular.

I decided to create a local interest group called Tayside open learning association (TOLA). I wrote to every educational institution in the area and we soon had over fifty members. We met monthly for seminars, presentations and open discussion. The local institutions provided accommodation and some even gave us refreshments. We charged a nominal membership fee for a regular newsletter. I was chairperson for the first three years and then stood down, but I remained on the committee. The association thrived and was a great way of networking and sharing ideas. Colleagues from Aberdeen and Grampian followed suit and created GOLA.

By now, we all had computers on our desks and stored material on floppy discs. We were delighted that technology now allowed us to change fonts, create new layouts and add pictures. Desktop publishing had arrived. I often printed overhead transparencies from my computer. The use of a digital projector to show slides directly from a computer was still in the future.

One morning in 1986 Andy put the mail on the table as I was having breakfast. I did not pay much attention as I ripped open the envelope and was amazed that it was a formal letter telling me I had been awarded an MBE. I had to keep it secret until the awards were announced on the Queen's birthday in June. I was invited to attend the ceremony at Buckingham Palace in November, but this clashed with a DipEdTech college block so I declined

Outside Buckingham Palace after my MBE investiture, with dad and Andy

and was given a new date in December. The Scottish Office paid for travel and accommodation for me and two guests, and Andy and my Dad accompanied me to a nice hotel in London. I was sad that I was only allowed two guests at the investiture, so I forced my parents to choose which of them attended. A colleague from the drama department taught me how to curtsey and I bought a pink hat and blouse to go with my smart grey suit. This time I did not wear pink tights. I was presented with my award by the Queen. She spoke to every recipient for exactly thirty seconds. When I said I was from Dundee she smiled and said she knew it, then she pushed my hand. This was my signal to step back and curtsey again. I was honoured to receive my gong but I have never had an occasion to wear it.

Flexibilities

For the annual AETT conference in 1987 I was asked to give a lecture on the resource implications of open learning. This sounded a rather dry topic, so I decided to develop a simulation. I had been to several events run by SAGSET (the unfortunate acronym of the Society for the Advancement of Gaming and Simulation in Education and Training) and I knew such experiences could be enjoyable and lead to powerful learning. I was not concerned with its designation as a game or simulation or simulation game, though some academics debated the merits of the terminology at great length.

There are many forms of open learning, depending on which aspects of flexibility are involved and organisers may choose which they want to implement. Some courses allow students to start and finish when they choose which is easy when all the resources are ready on the shelf. Others allow students to design their own form of assessment to demonstrate they have achieved their objectives.

I chose eleven aspects of flexibility and looked at their impact on six types of resource:

TRADITIONAL APPROACH > FLEXIBLE APPROACH

Set sequence of topics.	Variable sequence. Learner chooses route and topics.
Objectives and content are set in advance by the institution.	Learner negotiates objectives and content to suit their needs.
One pre-planned method of teaching.	Learner negotiates and selects methods of learning.
Prescribed entry requirements.	Open entry regardless of qualifications and experience.
Formal external examinations.	Learner negotiates timing and method of assessment.

Learners study on campus.	Learners choose where to study – at work, at home or on campus.
Fixed start date.	Learners may start at any time.
Fixed finish date.	Learners may finish at any time.
Seminars timetabled by tutor.	Tutor support available on demand.
Fixed attendance times, e.g. for practical work.	Learner attends centre when it suits them.
Support provided by college tutor.	Learner selects support from tutor, mentor, supervisor, colleague etc.

RESOURCE CARDS

Tutors	Academic staff to design materials and advise learners.
Materials	Learning packages in various media.
Facilities	Physical resources such as rooms and equipment.
Secretarial Support	Administration – often underestimated.
Institutional Support	Regulations and policies need to be flexible.
Favourable Attitudes	Change needs committed people.

The resources were represented by piles of coloured cards and the total number was fixed at the start. The resource cards were moved between committed resources and available resources during the simulation. Each flexible aspect was on a separate larger card with the resource implications given on the back. Participants were put into small groups to design a flexible learning system. They selected which cards they wanted then turned them over to see how many resources were needed and how many were released

---

Study on campus >>> learners choose where to study

- Materials will be needed for distance learning.
- Secretarial support will be needed to organise materials and keep records.
- Rooms will be made available for other uses.

Resources	Needed	Released
Tutors		
Materials	2	
Facilities		1
Secretarial Support	2	
Institutional Support		
Favourable Attitudes		

I designed it so that resources would be bound to runout, just like real life, and participants would be forced to prioritise their decisions. As with most simulations, the key learning took place in the small group discussions and the shared plenary analysis. Once people realised they could cluster the flexibilities together and choose which were most important, they could design a good course. Often they wanted to repeat the exercise using a different programme. I was interested to note which resources ran out; it surprised the participants to realise how important secretarial support and favourable attitudes were to the success of an open learning scheme.

The workshop was very successful, and SCET offered to publish it. It was called Flexibilities. They created a smart plastic folder with coloured laminated cards, OHP transparencies and a leader's guide giving different variations. It sold well at £25 per pack and they produced another version in Italian. I did quite well out of the royalties, and I used it as a training resource for many years. We considered creating an online version, but participants really enjoyed the physical movement of coloured cards.

Learning approaches are becoming more flexible and are allowing students more autonomy. But most formal higher education is still fairly rigid, as institutions are bound by validation criteria and cost implications. Staff often find ways to make their teaching more open, involving students in some of the decision making. Open learning is a powerful way to make education more accessible and inclusive.

Chapter Five

Northern College

Education seems full of mergers. Dundee College of Education merged with Aberdeen College of Education to become Northern College in 1987. This process also involved the merger of several departments. Many of the Dundee staff were unhappy with this arrangement as Aberdeen was the main campus and we felt like a subsidiary, less important part. In spite of the frequent use of teleconferencing and video conferencing, there was a massive amount of travel between the two centres.

I became the coordinator of tertiary education with responsibility for several courses and an overview of staff development. This gave me an increased salary and promotion to principal lecturer level. Some years later we split from Aberdeen and merged with the University of Dundee which does not have a principal lecturer post, so it looked as if I had been demoted to senior lecturer! Dundee University is again reorganising its structure and merging several departments; this may have logistical and financial advantages, but some staff members feel a loss of identity.

Northern College staff. I am in the front row,
five from the left.

I stood down as programme leader for the DipEdTech
to focus on my new responsibilities, but I continued as a tutor.
I wrote to all my colleagues thanking them for their support
and urging them to help the new leader in the same way. The
projectionist thanked me for my letter and said that he had
never before been thanked for doing his job. I put this sorry
state of affairs down to another example of academic snobbery
– many lecturers seemed to regard the support staff as lesser
beings and ignored them. I always passed the time of day with
all colleagues, and I received fantastic support from janitors
and secretaries alike.

The college introduced a staff development and career
review scheme (SDCR), and I was heavily involved in the
design of the process and the documentation and delivering of
the training. Staff had to review their own progress and have
an interview to discuss any issues, identify any training needs
and set future targets. The next year started with a review of
the targets. The processes of reflecting on the last year and
action planning are valuable, but there were some flaws in the
scheme. If your interviewer was your line manager, you may
be reluctant to mention any problems. If your interviewer was

not your line manager, they had no power to change your workload or organise training.

I was asked to set up a voluntary mentoring scheme for the academic staff. This was to create a confidential relationship that would offer support and challenge. I planned the system, trained the staff, and monitored and evaluated the process. I ensured a positive ethos by providing training and support for mentees as well as mentors. Several lecturers chose to have a mentor from the other campus, as this provided a degree of distance to discuss sensitive issues. The reactions were very positive with clear gains for mentees, mentors and the institution. Nevertheless, the pilot scheme was dismissed by senior management as "one of Gaye's touchy-feely ideas". I was upset and hurt by this comment, but not surprised.

I organised several staff development events, both in-house and using external experts. I remember one session which was for all academics and involved a lovely lunch. As I introduced the afternoon speaker I said something like *I hope you all enjoyed your lunch*. It had been a very good lunch with a very alcoholic sherry trifle and the staff had liked it so much they burst into spontaneous applause. I turned to the college secretary who had responsibility for the catering staff and said "Please would you convey that clap to the kitchen staff." He looked horrified and I realised what I had said, and everyone began to laugh. The giggles spread like a wave towards the back of the hall as people noted what I had said. The secretary made some tongue-in-the-cheek comment about being the health and a safety officer so he could not spread disease. For the next few days, wherever I went people passing me in the corridor clapped and laughed.

Another of my responsibilities was to read out some of the names at graduation. I checked the correct pronunciations, especially of the international students, and noted them phonetically on my programme. I always allowed plenty of time for each student to have their moment of glory. I announced the name and waited until they had walked across the platform received their award and walked off the other side of the stage. Only then did I read the next name. All other speakers announced the next name as soon as the student moved away from the principal. I thought that after three years of hard work each person deserved a minute as the focus of their celebration.

All universities are concerned about academic honesty, and many firms now offer "essays" for sale. Students submit essays electronically and the sophisticated software checks for plagiarism against the work of other students, electronic books and journals on the internet. My courses have largely managed to avoid the chance of plagiarism as our assignments are related to the students' real experiences which are specific and detailed. The best way to stop plagiarism is to design assessment methods that do not support it. But other courses often ask students for general essays that can easily be copied. If students are found guilty of plagiarism, the penalties can be high. They may have to redo the assignment, retake the module at their own expense, or have their whole course terminated. I had to investigate several cases of suspected plagiarism and it was usually fairly easy to distinguish the deliberate cheats from those who were struggling with how to write academic essays. Many students would rush an assignment and copy key ideas from the internet without noting their origin. They would then forget which parts were their own work. We provided training on how to find sources, how to acknowledge them and how to reference them correctly.

If students fail an assignment they can claim special consideration if there are good reasons and be allowed to re-submit. However, allowable circumstances are quite strict and do not include outside pressures. Consider the following two scenarios:

Case 1 is a twenty-year-old full-time student, who is not well motivated and only came to university to join their mates. They spent a lot of time socialising and they failed an assignment.

Case 2 is aged forty and is a part-time distance learner doing an in-service professional course while looking after two children and an elderly parent. They have been given extra responsibility at work due to a colleague's illness. They do not wish to submit sub-standard work so they do not hand anything in. It is clear to their tutor that an extra couple of weeks would be sufficient for them to complete the assignment satisfactorily.

My sympathy would be with the second case, and I would allow extra time for a non-penalty resubmission. This is against the letter of the regulations which do not allow for the impact of external factors, only for certificated medical issues.

When students were "terminated" because they had failed more than one assignment, they had the chance to appeal and provide evidence about extenuating circumstances. The appeals committee heard some terrible stories of genuine problems and we were usually sympathetic if students had put in place systems to prevent repeated failure. We were less convinced by appeals from a student's mother saying how hard they would work in the future.

I remember two cases that were not approved. I do not like attendance registers since mere presence does not necessarily lead to any learning. But some professional bodies require a minimum level of attendance before students are allowed on placement, and visa conditions for some international students have to be monitored. One student was being terminated for failing to attend half of the required classes. Her excuse was that she could not find her way to the lecture theatre even though it was always in the same room. Another student explained that his car had broken down and that was why he missed two weeks of his placement. He submitted the garage bill as evidence.

The first time I was asked to be an external examiner for a PhD I was nervous, but the student's supervisor assured me that this was a straightforward "middle-of-the-road" thesis which would be good to cut my teeth on. The topic was resource-based learning, and the candidate had visited three institutions and produced analytical case studies. However, they made no attempt to draw any conclusions or recommendations from the studies. I felt it was a competent piece of work at master's level, but not at doctoral standard. I asked an experienced colleague to give me a second opinion and was pleased that he concurred with my assessment. At the viva I tried to get the student to make some generalisations or to suggest how the ideas in their thesis could be implemented in their own organisation. But the candidate was not able to do so. My discussion with the internal examiner who was also the supervisor was uncomfortable to say the least, but he agreed that it could not pass. Indeed, it was so far off the mark that we could not ask for revisions as there was no evidence in the thesis or the oral of doctoral thinking. We failed the thesis, awarding a compensatory master's degree. The student complained and it went to their academic scrutiny process, and I was relieved when my decision was upheld. I felt sorry for the student as they had obviously had inadequate supervision; the work was not ready to be submitted. The student complained about the lack of support and was subsequently given another supervisor in another department and did eventually gain a doctorate.

I was surprised a couple of years later that the same supervisor asked me to examine another doctoral thesis, this time from a distance learner. The thesis was adequate but I felt there was a complete section missing and in the pre-meeting, the supervisor agreed. This was the main area for discussion in the viva and the student admitted that this was a major omission and that more field work would be needed, but they had run out of time. The student then said he was only in the UK for a few weeks, just enough time for the viva, to make a few revisions and then to graduate. This was in my opinion another example of inappropriate supervision. The candidate was not ready to submit, but I would not compromise my standards so they had to return overseas, complete the study, add a new section to the thesis and resubmit. This time, six months later, it was a good piece of work and worthy of a doctorate.

I was invited to examine an internal doctoral candidate at another university. I was sent detailed guidelines, and I was so impressed I introduced some aspects of the procedures to our own academic standards committee. One feature was that each examiner had to provide a written report in advance, which we would only share on the day of the viva. I sent in my report which was very favourable but with some issues for discussion and arrived in time for the meeting. The chairman announced that we may not be able to proceed as he was not sure if the candidate was eligible. I expressed my concern. Surely if the candidate was not eligible, she should not have been allowed to submit and I should not have been asked to read the thesis and travel across the country. After some debate, a very senior manager was summoned and after a private conflab, we were allowed to proceed. The viva went well and we all agreed that with very minor changes she should graduate with a doctorate. I did not understand the problem, but I did wonder if internal politics were involved. Fortunately my subsequent experiences of assessing and supervising doctorates were much happier for all.

BA in Professional Development

Judith George, Depute Director of the Open University in Scotland, told us about some exciting new degrees being offered at Alverno Community College in Wisconsin. Regardless of the content, they were based on developing eight abilities that they thought were essential for success at work and in life. These eight abilities are communication, problem solving, social interaction, effective citizenship, analysis, valuing, aesthetic engagement, and developing a global perspective. This was twenty years before the Curriculum for Excellence in Scotland identified four key capacities helping students become successful learners, confident individuals, responsible citizens and effective contributors. The Alverno curriculum focused on enhancing these skills in work-based settings and on personal development. This approach was inspiring, and the college set up a small group to design what became the BA in Professional Development (BAPD), and I was delighted to be involved.

In the late 1980s we set off for a country house hotel where we would spend the next two days in a planning meeting. The lion statues on the gateposts looked down with a hint of disapproval. After all, we four academics were going to design a new type of degree for mid-career professionals. It was to focus on context, process and outcomes rather than content. We hoped that by analysing, reflecting on and creating authentic work situations, the students would develop a range of complex relevant transferable skills. We wanted them to show personal growth, enhance the interactions with their colleagues, impact on their organisations and lead to the development of policy. Over the next quarter of a century through a range of inspired learning activities, inspiring tutors and inspirational students, we did just that. I think I hear the stone lions purring now.

Although most of the input for the BAPD was by distance learning, either by structured booklets or online modules, workshops were always an important feature. We ran regular workshops on campus and also online using various video conferencing platforms. These events were not compulsory and some students were never able to join them, but they were popular. They allowed students to meet each other and to have detailed discussions with their tutors, thus partly offsetting the isolation often felt by distance learners.

The BAPD was a part-time distance learning work-based qualification. Participants used their own workplace in which to enhance their skills of management, leadership, communication and so on. They carried out research, implemented new ideas, evaluated their practice and reflected on the whole experience. The degree was based around ten capabilities which were developed in discussion with the students:

- To apply knowledge and skills in practice
- To communicate effectively to a range of audiences
- To plan and organise systematically and responsively
- To analyse and evaluate challenging situations
- To solve complex problems
- To take responsibility for collaboration with others
- To behave in a professional and ethical way
- To apply principles and practices of equality and inclusion
- To evaluate aspects of practice of yourself and others
- To manage change and uncertainty

The course materials were printed booklets which contained interactive tasks. In later years they were replaced by online learning modules using a virtual learning environment (VLE) called Blackboard. The role of the tutors was to introduce the students to generic approaches and methods, and work with them in a consultative manner as they applied them to their own professional situation in which they were the expert. The assignments and projects for their degree were not just authentic assessments but real-life situations. The students included healthcare professionals, social workers, FE lecturers, volunteer managers and community workers, and their jobs impacted significantly on the lives of their students, clients, patients and colleagues. I found working with them was humbling and rewarding.

In the early years the course was very flexible, with students able to choose their own timetable and select from a

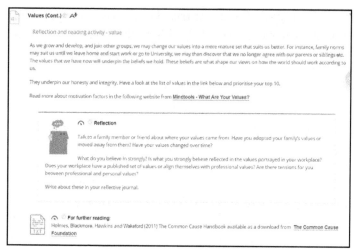

Screenshot from a BAPD module.

wide range of modules. We kept paper mastercopies in the storeroom and made a photocopy when a student requested it. A decision was made by senior management to reduce the number of modules available, and over half of the master copies were removed and destroyed. This was done without the knowledge of any of the tutors, leaving us to explain to angry students why their options were suddenly no longer available. Writing about this now, decades later, I am still furious. Not only did this interfere with the students' learning plans, but it disregarded our professionalism by not even consulting us about the decision. At least now, we would have an electronic version available!

On holiday in Austria with my husband, we had a tour guide who was very ineffective. She knew very little about local facilities and did not listen to the needs of her clients. She casually asked my husband what I did and he explained about the BAPD, saying how it could improve the profession-al competence of anyone. I could almost hear him adding *sotto voce* "Even you!" But it was true. I could have introduced her to tools that would have helped her with time management, listening skills, organisation of events and creating a database of local resources.

I remember a young Greek social worker who was in charge of personal care workers in Athens. I tutored her on her first module and had frequent phone calls to Greece, usually to try to boost her confidence since she was doing an amazing job with limited resources. Eventually her evaluations and reflections led to the obvious conclusion that her systems were very effective. She completed her degree and then took a PhD, again at a distance. Chryssi came over to Dundee to receive her doctorate at a graduation ceremony, and she rushed up to me and gave me a hug and said that my initial support had been crucial in giving her the confidence to continue.

One important feature of the BAPD was the importance it granted to learning from previous experience. It was quite common for students to gain credit against the learning outcomes of a module if they could reflect on their experience and show how they had met each of the objectives. Often this needed as much work as just taking the module, although the fees were less. But the BAPD also allowed students to provide evidence and a reflective commentary set against the ten capabilities to give credit equivalent to half an academic year. This saved considerable time and money. I tutored many students as they completed their APEL (Accreditation of Prior Experiential Learning) claim. The key was to focus on learning from experience, not just the experience itself. Once they grasped that, they were often amazed at how much they had learned as they carried out their job and how well they had transferred ideas from one context to another. I have also found while writing this book that I had forgotten many experiences and the impact they had on my personal learning and professional development.

One student, who was a practice manager in a busy dental surgery, gave an account of an autistic child with severe learning difficulties who had been brought in by her mother for a routine check-up. While they waited in the busy waiting room the child became so distressed that it was impossible for the dentist to examine her. When the student reflected on the whole experience, she identified several aspects to the problem and some ways to improve matters. She booked a new appointment at the start of the day when it was quieter and set up a couple of chairs in the storeroom as an extra waiting area with no other patients. She informed the dentist about the child's problems so he could allow extra time and could explain what he was going to do before he started. The student then realised that there were general implications from this scenario. She tried to ensure that the practice knew about any special needs of the patients before they arrived. She made parents aware of the facility to book an appointment at a quiet time and to wait in a private area. She organised staff training on working with autistic and very nervous patients. The analytical account she wrote related to several capabilities and the evidence of her experiential learning included a thank you letter from the mother, a copy of new notices on display in reception, a programme of the staff training event, and a comment from the General Dental Council's quality assurance inspector.

Another student gave an example of much more personal learning. He had disciplined an employee for being drunk at work, but subsequently found out the person was quite ill and had responded badly to a change in her medication. The student thought hard about his assumptions and behaviour and realised he had acted in a manner that was not professional or ethical. He also noted that the employee was from an ethnic minority group, so he wondered if he was racially discriminatory. He enrolled on an online course on "unconscious bias" and made a positive effort to put his learning into practice on a daily basis.

One of my BAPD students became very ill just before completing his final project. By chance I had also tutored him on another course, so I knew him quite well. He had a rapid-onset progressive illness that made it impossible for him to work or study. This was devastating for him, his wife and young family. I wondered if it would be possible to grant him an aegrotat degree. This comes from the Latin for "he/she is ill," and allows a qualification to be awarded if the candidate was deemed able to do the work but was prevented by illness. I asked if he would like me to explore the possibility and he was delighted as it gave him a positive focus. I then approached the university. They did not have an aegrotat policy; in fact, most people had never heard of it, although it was available in other universities. Once it had been approved by the various committees, I obtained medical evidence from the student and received agreement from the external examiner. Then I prepared a special case for the exam board which agreed to the award, subject to approval by senate which followed. The student's name appeared in the graduation booklet, but he was not well enough to attend the ceremony. I took his parchment and a copy of the booklet to his home and awarded him his degree. I donned my academic gown and hood, which seemed a little incongruous as he was in pyjamas. His wife and I toasted his success with lemonade. It was one of the proudest moments of my academic career.

I have always been involved in reflection, both for personal practice and as a topic I have taught. It is a key process in many of the courses I have run. There are many models of reflection, but I created my own which I published. I focused on both specific and general aspects of the situation. So in this case, specific reflection led to getting a degree for a particular student, while general reflection led to a change in university policy.

One of the most frustrating aspects of working in higher education (or perhaps in any career) is when managers make the wrong decisions because they had not listened to the staff who knew more about the issues than they did. They ignored our experience and discounted our professionalism. As part of an economy drive, we were told to merge the BAPD with the BA in Childhood Practice. The two staff teams already shared ideas and good practice, but the two courses were very different – although both were by distance learning for in-service mid-career participants. The BACP was validated by SSSC (the Scottish Social Services Council), and students had to meet their competences. The merger meant that BAPD students had to follow these requirements too, adding an unnecessary complication and restriction on their learning. We complained bitterly that this was inappropriate and, after fifteen months, the bean-counters relented and the courses were separated. It was very stressful for the staff, confusing for the students, and a waste of time and resources.

We franchised the BAPD to a college in Belfast (now Belfast Metropolitan College) and built up a very supportive relationship over the years. I was part of the original team applying for validation by Northern College and the Open University Validation Services, who had replaced CNAA as the degree-awarding body. The applicant team from Dundee and the validating team not only stayed in different hotels in Belfast, but travelled in separate planes. About fifteen years earlier I had refused to travel to the province. In the seventies I was often invited to give staff development seminars in other colleges. I was told it was quite safe: a car would meet my plane, and take me to the institution. I would give my talk and the car would return me to the airport and I would only be in the country for three hours. I was not even invited to lunch. This whirlwind tour did not inspire confidence, so I pleaded a prior engagement. I did feel a little guilty, but I had no connection with them and so felt no responsibility. Visiting Belfast for several days on a couple of occasions as part of my involvement in the BAPD was quite different. It was my job and I was happy to oblige.

After the rounds of inquisition, the applicant team normally waited in an adjacent room for about an hour to hear the outcome, but our Belfast colleagues had other ideas. They took us off to a nearby pub and plied us with whisky. By the time we returned to hear the fortunately positive result we were quite merry.

A few months later, I returned to provide some staff development workshops for the new Belfast tutors on the delivery and assessment of the modules. We used some existing assignments, and spent time analysing them and assigning grades and comments. One evening a

BAPD validation in Belfast.

colleague and I went to see the Bolshoi Ballet giving a magical performance at the Waterside Theatre. We were shown around the city, full of reminders of the troubles. Some hotels had been bombed many times. There were poignant murals on the end walls of buildings. The college had several sites, and often had to repeat courses in more than one venue to satisfy the demand for equal provision for different religious groups.

Many of the students at Belfast Met were policemen whose role in the province had changed from being almost military to more like community workers. They were keen to learn more about topics such as leadership, collaborative working, volunteering and mentoring. Quite a few used the BAPD as a stepping stone into postgraduate study, and enrolled with our university for part-time masters and doctoral degrees by distance learning.

The BAPD developed another interesting collaborative relationship and that was with the Ministry of Health in Eritrea in North East Africa. The University of Dundee taught nurses and also managers, largely by distance learning but supported by in-country visits. A colleague and I went to Eritrea for a week in March 2007 to provide support for students on the BAPD. This initiative was part of a joint Ministry of Health-sponsored programme to build the capacity of key staff in Eritrea, and we held several meetings with senior officials about possible future plans and collaborations.

My colleague planned to do a team building exercise and during a stopover at Frankfurt he tried in vain to buy a set of Lego bricks. Instead he decided that the small drinking cups on the plane would be useful as building blocks. So he persuaded me and two other passengers to bring a few cups back each time we visited the toilet. He stuffed them all into his holdall and was relieved it was not opened by customs.

The exercise was so successful that one of the students asked to keep the paper cups as a training resource. We had to declare how much money we had on arrival, keep receipts for all spending, and show how much we had remaining when we left. I think this was to stop money entering the country illegally.

We had been briefed about the happy disposition of the Eritreans. The phrase "their default setting is a smile" captures precisely the positive and friendly attitude of our students and of all the locals we met. The people impressed me with their resilience. After thirty years of war, they were so optimistic and dynamic. Asmara, the capital, is a big bustling city with wide streets. It is hot, dry and dusty. Some parts are opulent with beautiful buildings, but some areas are much poorer. The internet was unreliable and would sometimes be off for days at a time. When it was restored the internet cafés would be full. There were many faiths, but they were Eritrean first. When I entered the large church in Asmara I felt an overwhelming sense of peace and lightness. I immediately sat on a pew and prayed.

One of the nurses invited us to her home for a coffee ceremony. The coffee beans are first shown to each guest, then they are roasted and each guest smells the aroma, and finally everyone gets to drink the coffee. I asked for tea with milk in a café, and was bemused that it came with a jug of hot milk. After that I stuck to black tea. We needed special permission to be allowed out of Asmara to visit some hospitals. The pass was only valid for one day, and our minibus was stopped and checked twice by armed police. The toilets were mostly holes in the ground inside a shed. Outside was a bucket and a water tap for flushing. As a kindness to visitors, the locals would fill the bucket and flush the toilet before we used it.

Our students were 16 senior healthcare executive managers from all parts of the country, and some were from very remote areas

Our Eritrean BAPD students.

with extreme communication problems. Their work related to a range of management issues including finance, personnel, training, health promotion, quality control, record keeping, and managing resources such as pharmaceuticals and blood products. They were mature, highly committed and motivated and very responsive in class. It was a delight to work with them.

We used an adult learning approach to running the workshops involving much participation by the students. We introduced a variety of interactive methods using games, simulations, role play, problem solving and group work. They worked individually, in pairs and in small groups. We presented general principles which they contextualised and applied to their unique working situations. We used their real examples as a starting point to explain the underlying theoretical bases. We adopted a range of teaching styles to suit the mix of learning styles within the group. Within the workshops we created formative tasks which they used to build towards their summative assignments.

Our first activity was using a collection of objects in a bag. I held up a coin and asked the question "Why is this object like a good manager?" My answer referred to the fact that it had a face value, but this was a coin from ten years ago so the purchasing power was a lot less. A good manager needed to be aware of values and to know that they could change over time. Also, the coin had two faces and a good manager needed to see different perspectives. I then invited them each to take an object out of the bag and discuss within small groups why it was like a good manager. We shared a few examples in plenary. All the objects were specially purchased items related to Dundee or Scotland, such as a pen, tea towel, fridge magnet, tartan purse, and mug. Once they had explored the managerial characteristics I explained that they could keep the item as a gift from Dundee. They were delighted. I have used this activity many times with different questions: "What makes a good university teacher?" or "How can this help you improve your wellbeing?" I have a large collection of about fifty unusual objects that I have accumulated for the purpose, and several colleagues regularly borrowed my bag of objects.

Through a range of structured processes of student-led activities, they were able to develop core abilities which enhanced their confidence and professional competence. We encouraged them to think explicitly about the processes as well as the content of the modules and to become lifelong learners. They were also able to plan ways to communicate more effectively with their colleagues and teams. We helped them plan projects, and were keen to introduce them to professional ethics when working with clients and data. We talked about confidentiality and informed consent, and one participant suddenly announced that he now realised that a visitor who led a project a year before had not behaved ethically towards him or his colleagues. We have had some problems with getting ethical approval for our students' projects, as the process takes so long that they do not have enough time to carry out the investigation before the

Group activity.

submission date. At other times, staff have been frustrated by being told they need approval from the ethics committee for the most basic of communications. I do not think we should need sanction to ask students or colleagues their opinions if we simply want to gather some ideas, without quoting the views or identifying individuals. Some colleagues disagree.

The students were involved in substantial roles within the country. One was responsible for setting up a national blood bank, but found that he had a health education issue as a main problem. Many members of the public had heard about the link between blood and AIDS and feared that if they donated blood, they would be exposed to HIV. In one hospital we visited, we saw relatives waiting to give blood transfusions to an ill patient as only blood from family members was deemed to be safe. A similar health education issue had a negative impact on a government initiative to reduce the impact of malaria. People were provided with disinfectant for their bed nets to repel mosquitos. But they did not use the disinfectant, as they did not understand the relationship between mosquitos and malaria.

One morning the class was very subdued, and they told us that the father of one of them had died and they would all

Health education poster.

go to the funeral later that day. This was sad for them, but also confusing for the visiting lecturers. Were we expected to attend as a measure of respect, or would that be an intrusion? We decided that since we did not have appropriate clothes and did not know the format of the funeral, we might do more harm than good. When they returned to class the following day, including the bereaved person who did not want to miss any more of our course, we expressed our condolences.

I spent much of the time working with individual students and giving detailed feedback on their work. Their line manager asked me to identify any students who were struggling with these formative tasks so he could arrange for them to have extra study time. This gave me a dilemma. Although his intentions were supportive, I did not feel I could or should tell him about the progress or difficulties of the students. The contract was between student and tutor, and the details should be confidential. I continued to give tutor support by email once we were back in Dundee. The participants wrote short accounts referring to academic literature and linking the topic to their own situation. The content of their writing was usually fine and comprehensible, but there were often problems with the language. I identified the main issues and rewrote one paragraph to give them an example. I do not think it is the role of the tutor to act as a proof-reader. Many of them made similar grammatical mistakes, so I compiled a detailed list and sent it to everyone.

Eritreans loved sweets, and we had been warned to arrive with peppermints and shortbread as gifts for the office staff. There was also a local tradition that we bought some luxurious gateaux from the hotel on the last day of the course. These confections were displayed in the common area and everyone came; not just the tutors and students, but anybody in the vicinity who was keen to enjoy the treat. When we left the hotel I packed my case and left a half-finished pack of biscuits and some teabags behind, hoping the staff would make use of them. But the porter came rushing down thinking I had forgotten them until I explained he could keep them.

Although there were several computers for individual use, there was only one laptop used for class presentations. It was shared between two courses and was in high demand. I decided to buy them another laptop and donate it to the centre. I discussed the ideal specification with the technologist and arranged for the purchase to be channelled through the British Council office. I ordered it as soon as I returned to Dundee. I had stated that my gift should be anonymous, but a few months later a colleague visited and took a photograph of the new laptop adorned with a note: "Kindly do-

Cakes from the hotel.

nated by Dr Gaye Manwaring". At the final evaluation meeting we were each presented with a traditional earthenware coffee set. It was a thoughtful gift, but I worried that the bulk and weight might cause problems with my baggage allowance on the flight home. We travelled overnight and had the luxury of business class, so our seats fully reclined meaning we could sleep. When we arrived at Frankfurt with several hours to wait, we enjoyed the delicious free food in the lounge and I was delighted to be able to have a shower.

A year later one, of the senior managers from Eritrea asked us to arrange a study tour for him visiting educational institutions in Scotland. So we began to organise a programme. Then we received notification from a senior UK government official that this person would not be granted a visa and we should not entertain him. Apparently he had moved his family out of Eritrea on holiday, and the totalitarian regime thought he might take this opportunity to escape.

Teaching Qualification in Further Education

We offered a teaching qualification to lecturers in further education colleges, and I was the programme leader. We ran undergraduate and postgraduate versions, and within a few years we were the biggest provider in Scotland and worked with colleges across the land. The General Teaching Council was pressurising FE colleges to get all their staff qualified, so we had a captive market. We created a distance learning course using structured booklets and tutor support. We also ran a few face-to-face workshops where students could meet colleagues from other colleges and share ideas. We also had to visit the colleges and observe the students teaching. We

worked closely with
the staff development
officers in the colleges
who also had an as-
sessment role. Our
staff were experienced
at writing self-study
materials and provid-
ing tutor support and
formative feedback on

FE students on a golf course
design programme.

assignments. So we became a popular provider, and many colleges chose to use our course. Some individual students in colleges who used other providers wanted to pay their own fee
and come to us, but this was blocked as teaching observations
had to be arranged by their college.

I loved visiting the FE colleges to observe the lecturers.
The observations were a formal part of their assessment, and I
always found them enlightening. I had the privilege of watching students being taught how to mark out the white lines on
a sports field, how to carry out tree surgery safely and how to

design a golf
course, including
such details as
how to estimate
how much sand
you needed to fill
a bunker.

I saw how
a catering lecture
averted a near
disaster. One of
his students was

FE tree surgery students.

137

preparing a meal for paying guests in the college's restaurant, when he noticed that the food on the grill was on fire. The lecturer did not act on the fire hazard himself but calmly informed the student and then watched how she dealt with it. He then told the student to go and explain to the customers why their meal would be delayed. This made such a powerful learning experience for the student, and also for the whole class when they discussed it later.

While visiting a small rural college I noticed a dog in the classroom. It was quiet and well-behaved, but did not appear to be a guide dog. I asked the lecturer about it and he explained that it was a companion for a vulnerable student who was lacking in confidence and would only attend class if he could bring his dog. The lecturer had ascertained that no one in the class was allergic to dogs and nobody objected to its presence. In fact, the class members looked after the dog whenever the owner had to leave the class. Over time, the student grew in confidence, gained his qualification and was able to apply for jobs without his constant canine companion.

Many colleges offered courses on independent living for students with learning difficulties. The lecturers used creative methods to help the students. They set up a mock kitchen so the students could learn the difference between products that might appear similar. We take for granted that we know which polish to use on furniture or shoes or brass ornaments, but it is not so easy for a shy, illiterate person. The catering staff were incredibly patient and supportive when helping such students choose their lunch and pay for it.

Rossie School on the East coast of Scotland provides care for vulnerable children. It has secure accommodation in what used to be called an "approved school". One of the staff taught horticulture and enrolled on the TQFE, and I went to observe his teaching. The atmosphere in the school was bright and positive, but it still felt like a prison as doors were locked behind me every few yards. It may be different now. I saw the students' lounge and was told there was no TV as two nights ago they had broken it up into pieces small enough to be posted through the bars (about four inches apart) onto the garden below. The class I observed was about taking root cuttings. As I watched a tall 16-year-old boy wield a very sharp knife, I remembered I had been told he was there for murder. The staff worked with students on an individual basis to help them achieve their full potential. One of the successes of the horticulture course was the growing of culinary herbs which were sold to the local shops and restaurants.

Another FE lecturer who worked in a prison ran courses on maths and English for a group of sex offenders. They were kept separate from the other inmates. The lecturer told me that he focused on the topic of the lesson and how to help his learners. He did not think about why they were in prison. One of the inmates told him that he was the only member of staff who did not treat him with contempt. He said the lecturer did not ask what he had done nor why and did not judge him, but treated him as a human being who still had potential to achieve. This lesson in self-esteem probably had more impact than any of the official curriculum.

I was constantly impressed by how much the lecturers cared about their subject and their students. Sadly, the same cannot always be said for university lecturers, some of whom resent having to teach students as it diverts time away from their research. It is still much more strenuous to become qualified to teach in FE than in HE. FE staff were keen to focus on employability and to equip the students for a productive career. So health and beauty students were taught people skills for working with clients and staff, and financial skills for managing a small business as well as how to colour hair or paint nails. They learned their practical skills on mannequins before trying them on fellow students, and then they beautified members of the public under supervision by their tutors. Painters and decorators were trained in a mock house with many small rooms so they could practice painting and wallpapering around radiators and electric sockets. They often had to deal with conflicting advice from the lecturers and their placement employers; the college might tell them to use three undercoats, while the employer in the real world might say that one was enough. Often employers would look for future employees among the students on placement. The colleges were keen to ensure the students developed and demonstrated appropriate soft skills such as politeness, punctuality, reliability and honesty, as well as meeting the professional standards of the industry.

At the same time, I was also a tutor on a degree in professional development. We arranged a creative link between the two courses so that the credits from the undergraduate TQFE could be used within the framework of the BAPD degree, thus saving a lot of time and money. Credits from the postgraduate TQFE could be used within our Master's programmes. As e-learning became more prominent we revised the TQFE and created an online programme. The content delivery and assignments were done online, but we still visited the students to observe them in action.

Staff Development and Appraisal

The Scottish Office Education Department funded and supported many major national initiatives focused on school improvement. Some of these projects were highly contentious and were likely to be challenged by stakeholders, all of whom had to be persuaded of their value. Sensitive preparation was needed as much as quality training.

I was involved in several varied topics over the years such as health education, mentoring, and the Scottish qualification for headship. The most significant and largest project was staff development and appraisal (SDA) for school teachers, and I was part of the so-called "A Team" which included staff from colleges, local authorities, schools and the inspectorate. It occupied a significant part of my time from 1989 for about six years. The Scottish Office paid the college for my time at a very high rate, and I did not know whether to feel valued or insulted when I was called a "cash cow" by a senior college colleague.

Part of the initial research involved us visiting a lot of firms to find out about their appraisal systems. They were very generous and shared documents and case studies. I soon realised that careful introduction of the scheme was essential if staff were not to feel threatened. I visited insurance companies, manufacturers, utilities, government organisations, universities and banks. The high point was a visit to the HQ of a bank, where I had lunch in the executive dining room. I had been given a gin and tonic before eating, so I declined the wine and brandy. But my host insisted on giving me a bottle of wine (with its own corporate label) to take home.

We collated our findings into a report which summarised the advantages for the organisation, the managers and the staff. These included good motivation, improved communication, and clarification of roles. But we also discussed the possible pitfalls of credibility, negative attitudes, and lack of follow-through. This is an excerpt from the report:

> All stressed the importance of ensuring that staff development and appraisal should be seen by staff as non-threatening. Consultation should take place with staff at every stage. The most common advice was to present appraisal first and foremost as being about development and certainly not as a mechanism for eliminating poor performers. The systems had to be seen to produce something. The benefits had to be clear to all staff, who needed to be given some sense of ownership of the scheme.

We spent the first year designing and piloting the training materials which eventually amounted to several large blue ring binders of printed materials as well as video and interactive video resources. The materials covered methods of self-evaluation and collecting evidence that a teacher would use before an SDA interview, how the interviewer would analyse the material, detailed examination of the interview process, and follow-up staff development plans. Additional resources included specific examples from primary and secondary schools, and case studies of teachers going through the process.

We used the cascade model, so we trained a couple of teachers from each school who then delivered the training to the rest of their colleagues. We used a single drop cascade which can be very effective, but beyond that the message often gets diluted.

SDA celebration cake.

Over a period of several years, a team of thirty College of Education lecturers delivered training to representative teachers from every primary and secondary school in Scotland. Each course lasted for three days in a luxury hotel, a reward for the hard work the participants did. The hotels were chosen from across Scotland to provide a consistent level of facilities to cater for large groups and small break-out areas. The food was wonderful and most venues had a swimming pool and gym, as well as a bar that was usually occupied well into the night. One course started on Shrove Tuesday and, when we pointed this out to the hotel catering staff, they gave us pancakes as well as our normal desserts and set up a mobile kitchen to teach participants to make (and toss!) pancakes. I was on one of the SDA events when the Berlin Wall came down in November 1989. I remember watching the scenes on breakfast TV in my bedroom with tears pouring down my face. When we reached our century, we had a cake to celebrate one hundred courses made to look like one of the ring binders with blue and gold icing.

There were three trainers and about thirty participants on each course. Typically two trainers would deliver the course, while the third acted as evaluator, as well as reserve, "fixer" and runner between groups. Another trainer delivered materials to the hotel and cleared everything away at the end. As well as the training materials, interactive video discs and players there was a supplies box of basic stationery and post-its, Blu-Tack, a holepunch and stapler. These courses were challenging and hard work for trainers and participants alike. Course members were expected to deliver this same course within their schools to a potentially hostile audience.

On the third day of the course the regional advisers and directorate staff were invited to respond to local issues. "Appraisal" is an emotive word, and the whole initiative was met with some anxiety and even hostility by teachers and their unions. The scheme was meant to allow teachers and their managers to evaluate and evidence their practice and identify areas of weakness so they could be remedied by additional training or extra resources or changes in working styles. But some feared it would lead to disciplinary action or lack of promotion. Others were concerned that not enough time would be allowed for the process, and that there would not be enough money or time for any identified training needs. The anxieties were understandable and were similar to those expressed about the SDCR scheme in the colleges. So our job was as much a public relations exercise as it was about training in the mechanics of the SDA scheme. As well as instruction in the details of SDA, we were aware that we were providing more transferable skills. We delivered using team teaching and modelled a facilitative and empowering approach. We demonstrated how to balance the focus of the task, the needs of the group, and at times the demands of an individual. We showed how to defuse a charged situation, respect genuine concerns and build self-esteem. We helped teachers develop sensitive interviewing skills and illustrated how to gather qualitative evidence about effective classroom practice.

This cascade approach to training meant we had a double agenda: the SDA process, and the way of delivering it to the rest of the school staff. We introduced some of the content, then put the teachers into pairs. Each pair was given a different section of the materials and had two hours to familiarise themselves with the content and plan their delivery to the rest of the group. The participants then gave feedback on the delivery. So by the end they had all experienced the whole package and had learned how to give feedback in a sensitive and constructive manner. This all sounds rather dire, but there was usually a lot of fun too. The teachers were creative in designing how to deliver their segments, and often included songs or poems. Some acted out scenarios, and the hotel staff were always most helpful in providing props.

We introduced a closing ceremony at the end of each course. Every participant was presented with the large blue binders containing all the materials they would need to deliver the training within their own school. Then we carried out the goodbye exercise. We asked the participants to close their eyes, and then said the following:

Over the last three days you have worked closely together and have supported each other through the process. I want you to imagine you are leaving, as you will do in a few minutes. Pick up your training materials, your overnight bags and your coat and walk out of the training room across the foyer. As you reach the front door of the hotel you realise that you did not say goodbye to your fellow participants and you wonder if they are still there. So you walk back across the foyer, enter the training room, put your materials and bags back on your seat. Everyone is still in the room so you now have the chance to say goodbye to each of them individually and to thank them for their collaboration. So open your eyes and say those farewells for real.

At that point people started milling around, thanking each other, shaking hands and hugging, laughing and sometimes crying. But it marked the ending in a powerful way.

This was a major staff development project that gave SDA training to teachers from every school in the country. The trainers learned a lot too. I developed my skills in facilitating the discussion of sensitive topics. With a gentle smile or a raised eyebrow, you can encourage the shy person to speak up and persuade the garrulous one to keep quiet. Putting people into small activity groups is a skill in itself. You can let participants organise themselves, but often you will want to ensure you have equal numbers and perhaps to mix people up. The commonest way is to give everyone a number and then put all those with number one in a group, ask all those with two to make another group, and so on. But I have seen a tutor who wanted to split a class of thirty into ten groups of three, but ending up with three groups of ten! Participants often grumble when put into groups, partly because they have to move and this may also involve moving a jacket, briefcase and cup of coffee. If there is room, have a semi-circle for plenary discussions with breakaway tables for groups round the outside. Since most of our courses were held in large hotel ballrooms, this was usually possible.

At the end of the SDA project I wrote to the team members, thanking them and sharing some of my memories:

- I was carried on a makeshift stretcher in the team-building exercise.
- I was asked for a tambourine needed in 30 minutes for a presentation, and managed to get one in time.
- I found the supplies box so useful I now have my own box complete with four-hole punch.
- I have only eaten blue icing three times – on those spectacular "manual" cakes.
- I really valued the sharing of resources, icebreakers and skills.
- I think we followed the basic principles of SDA: self-evaluation, focus on positive aspects, improve areas of concern, provide support, and value individuals.

I learned a great deal from the whole experience which I was able to transfer to new situations. I expressed this in a letter to the Scottish Office:

- I have used activities from the packs with other courses.
- I have used the videos for tutor training.
- I have incorporated the ideas of SDA into schemes and training for staff at Northern College and with community dentists.
- I have used the cascade model of dissemination in other projects.

- I have used my facilitation skills in other workshops.

I was delighted that the Scottish Office was also pleased with the results and I still have their official thank you letter, dated 22.3.95:

> ...My indebtedness to the A Team for keeping up with the original aims and for carrying through the visions and intentions, and to an exceptionally high level. Though the main thrust was to ensure delivery of training for the SDA programme, part of the strategy was to use the courses to attain other objectives. These included the provision of at least one member of staff in every school with an intense experience of exemplary training.

In addition to this standard letter, there was a handwritten postscript for me:

> I am particularly grateful to you for answering this challenge and taking the whole operation through with your own constant attention to detail. Many thanks.

Medical Open Learning Service (MOLS)

I was also seconded to another project. This was on medical education, and occupied about a day a week for six years. It was funded by the Scottish Council for Postgraduate Medical and Dental Education based in Edinburgh, and my role was to work with doctors to design training materials for general practitioners. The first item was an interactive booklet called "The Challenge of AIDS: A learning programme for general practitioners on HIV infection and AIDS", published in 1988. It contained factual information (correct at the time) with self-test questions and answers, and details of relevant organisations. There were also eight case studies about patients who might present at a surgery. These included a man who injected heroin, someone who had visited prostitutes and had read about AIDS in the press, a sexually active homosexual, and a police officer who had been covered in blood when assisting an intravenous drug user who had slashed her wrist. Each was followed by specific questions with comments overleaf. These were intended to stimulate personal reflection and also discussion with colleagues. Reading the text now, I am struck by similarities with Covid-19: test and trace; anxiety in the general population; some patients being asymptomatic; lack of knowledge about long-term effects.

In 1991 I was involved in redesigning a booklet on Learning General Practice to help doctors learn as much as possible from their practice. I introduced three approaches to learning: systematic, speculative and opportunistic. I wanted doctors to be able to learn from opportunities that occurred as well as from planned training events. This is an excerpt from the prologue:

I met three doctors who had been to a lecture on the management of elderly patients and I asked what they thought of it. Two said it had been very useful, but one found it a waste of time. Why the different views?

The first had a particular pressing problem and the lecturer had suggested several ways forward, so this person had identified his learning needs in advance and found a way of meeting them. The second had really attended to renew contact with colleagues, but she had related the lecture to her own practice and found it applied. The third had drifted into the lecture but listened passively and made no transfer of the ideas to his own practice.

However, on the way home the third person dropped in to visit a colleague at the local hospital. While he was waiting he overheard the secretary's phone calls. Clearly, the callers were not being helped either by the manner or the information supplied by the secretary. He also accepted that it was not all the fault of the secretary who obviously needed some training and support in telephone skills. He wondered how his own receptionist coped in his absence. He decided to investigate and if necessary to give her advice on how to deal with difficult callers.

All three doctors learned something that day that helped them be more effective at work. One organised his learning systematically, based on a planned learning event – the lecture. One reflected on the learning event and applied it to her own situation. One did not learn from the lecture at all, but took advantage of an unrelated incident and learned from it by reflection.

The next project was much larger. It was ACE (Active Continuing Education: a series of learning programmes for general practice). The materials were for individual or group study, and were delivered to every practice in Scotland. They were collated in ring binders containing interactive tasks, documents, audio tapes and photos. The materials were printed and packaged in the college. They were based on case studies of real patients, and I worked with four groups of GPs in different parts of Scotland. One group in Aberdeen could only meet after evening surgery so our discussions took place until 10.15 pm and then I caught the train to Dundee getting home at midnight.

The philosophy behind the learning packages was to encourage doctors to reflect on and discuss their decision-making strategies. The examples were genuine, but the activities encouraged them to apply them to their own context and to focus on general and transferable learning. Some of the doctors were keen to include unusual cases, but I insisted we needed examples that would seem relevant to other practices. This is from the introduction:

> This learning programme is written for general practitioners by general practitioners. It addresses common everyday issues in an attempt to provoke reflection and discussion. We started with the idea of "problem patients" and soon realised this label was inappropriate. Patients may have problems of many kinds, but the problem may be with the doctor or with the practice organisation. We all had problems, difficulties and dilemmas, but there are mechanisms and approaches to help us cope. We all try to learn from experience.

The packages were sent out in monthly instalments, and we suggested that they used them for discussion at staff meetings. The topics included conditions and dilemmas that are still current, unlike the AIDS material. Some of the questions were about medical treatment, while others were about management systems and ethics:

- An elderly confused patient wants to stay in her home but her daughter wants her sectioned for her own safety.
- A young mother is concerned about her baby but each visit is from a different doctor and the lack of continuity fails to identify the real problem.
- Some are about pain such as persistent headaches or shingles, and an intriguing case: "Knee pain and bankruptcy." The GP initially thought the pain was psychosomatic due to stress about finance; the patient was very depressed, but also had arthritis in his knees.
- Management of chronic conditions such as diabetes and arthritis, which can lead to social isolation as well having clinical symptoms.

I also introduced an action planning algorithm to help doctors respond to complex cases. It leads them through a series of questions and suggests a range of actions at each stage. It helps them clarify the detail of the problem, identify ways to seek for a possible solution, and examine useful resources. After implementing the solution, they evaluate it and consider learning points for the future. I adapted the tool to use in several other situations.

Patient confidentiality was assured, but there was one case where the lack of a name did not provide anonymity as the geographical location and the specific injuries of the patient had received exposure in the national press. A child had been severely injured in an accident and, when she was eventually discharged from hospital, the local surgery took over her care. She had lost one leg, had major internal injuries and was doubly incontinent. The practice had to devise a care plan for her complex medical, physical, social and psychological needs including anticipated changes during adolescence and adulthood. I sometimes wonder how she is coping now. We were able to gain the permission to use the example, as it gave rise to a valuable set of learning points.

One of the photos in another case study was of an elderly woman who had shingles on her buttocks. I was embarrassed one day to hear one of our printers calling out "Here are eight hundred photos of Gaye's bum!" The addition of colour photographs, detailed patient histories, test results, and recordings and transcripts of consultations added to the authenticity of the packages. I was pleased to note the distinctive green binder on the bookcase when I visited my own GP.

As a thank you, the council invited me and my husband to a special dinner at the Surgeons Hall in Edinburgh and I was one of the guests given a formal vote of thanks in the after-dinner speech. It was a wonderful meal in sumptuous surroundings and we had a great time. Andy did not own a dinner jacket so he had hired one, but when he got ready he found they had given him a dress shirt which was the wrong size. We phoned the shop and agreed to swap the shirt for the correct size as we drove to Edinburgh. We stopped on the outskirts of Edinburgh at the back of a car park for Andy to replace his tee shirt with the new dress shirt. We then discovered that the shirt required cufflinks, but all of Andy's were at home. I remember that a colleague lived on that side of the city, so we banged on his door. In response to my request that we were in a hurry but could we please borrow some cufflinks, he simply said, "Gold or silver?" A few days earlier Andy had sliced the top off his finger and the health centre nurse had shown him how to re-bandage it by using a little plastic guide tool. The surgeons at the dinner were most impressed with the neat bandage, even more so when Andy said he had done it himself.

As part of my role as director of the open learning service I also worked with community dentists, in part running workshops to support their teaching skills. The main difference for community dental officers was the greater need for excellent communication skills working with patients in their own homes and in local centres. I have worked with many people from the caring professions, most of them kind, competent and hard-working, but the community dentists that I met had an enhanced level of humanity and compassion. Many of their patients were elderly or had chronic health conditions, and I asked experienced officers to talk about some of their cases in the workshops. One reported that he had treated several patients who were dying from AIDS and were keen to have new dentures fitted before their death. He explained that this was not vanity but an attempt to recapture part of their personal identity. Another asked the audience how they would respond to the following situation that he had encountered. The elderly lady offered to make him some tea while he set up his equipment in her lounge. He had to go back to his car and saw her in the kitchen squatting over the washing up bowl and urinating in it before emptying the contents down the sink. He continued with the treatment but declined any refreshment.

I also ran a pilot for a continuing education programme in four health boards in the early 1990s. It had the following aims:

- To help dental officers develop their full potential and thus improve the effectiveness of the service.
- To provide a mechanism to identify and arrange suitable educational experiences.
- To provide early indication of any issues which might become professional problems later and to suggest solutions.

The scheme was a similar format to the SDCR process at Northern College. The focus was on staff development and was separate from discipline and promotion procedures. Dental officers and their reviewers each prepared documents that were discussed in an interview that led to an action plan. I organised training sessions before the cycles started. A range of training needs were identified that were normally met within that health board, usually in-house, although there were some cases of mutual exchange.

NEEDS   **ACTION PLANS**

Resuscitation update	Course on collapse and resuscitation
Delivery of dental health education	Local workshop on teaching methods
Confidence with geriatric patients	Course on care of the elderly
Management of handicapped patients	Secondment

Radiography management	Videos at postgraduate centre
Easier access to remote patients	Driving lessons

The evaluation was positive from the dental officers, the reviewers and the health boards, recognising clear gains with minimal cost and disruption. This was due in part to careful introduction of the scheme to explain and ensure that this was not appraisal under another name.

* * *

I was involved with many different groups acting as a consultant, an evaluator, a designer of materials or a trainer. I worked with Tulliallan Castle, the Scottish Police College. When we visited this marvellous gothic building, set in ninety acres of parkland, we were amazed at the ability of the recruits to eat a substantial three-course meal in just fifteen minutes. Was this training their gut to sit in a squad car and munch on unhealthy snacks? I worked with a colleague running some workshops on teaching methods and the design of learning materials. I was a senior lecturer and my colleague was a lecturer, so the Police College insisted on paying us different rates even though we were doing the same job. Fortunately the money went to our college, not to us personally. This reminds me of another example of hierarchical discrimination. When we moved into the new Dundee College of Education building, principal lecturers like John Clarke were given a glass-fronted bookcase while the rest of us had open bookshelves and dusty books. When John retired, the person who moved into his room was an unpromoted lecturer, so they took away the glass from his bookcase!

As the police trainers began to design training packages for themselves, we acted as editors. On one occasion I was driving home when I was stopped for speeding, but not too fast. I pointed to the back seat, which was full of training items with the Tulliallan logo clearly visible, and explained I was in a hurry to get on with my work for the police. They let me off with a gentle reprimand.

We were invited to run some workshops on teaching methods to the training officers at Castle Huntly, an open prison near Dundee. We arrived to start a session at 9.30am and had just begun when the alarm was sounded. The place was in lockdown and all the prison officers in our class were dispatched to help with the emergency. We found out later that an audit had shown that a knife was missing from break-fast. After a thorough search it was discovered hidden in a toilet cistern, to be sharpened up later as a weapon. So we were then able to resume our workshop.

Chapter Six

The University of Dundee

After twelve years, Northern College split and the two colleges merged with their local university. We became part of the University of Dundee and eventually moved into the city campus. Again, we felt like poor relations. Some of the senior executives did not want the merger, and few of our staff had doctorates which was the norm in other university departments. Our focus was on teaching, not on research. We were monitored by our professional bodies that validated our programmes, but these quality assurance regimens were different from those in the university so there were tensions. Since the university had its own staff development officer, that part of my role vanished. In practice I continued to carry out a lot of staff development work, especially for new lecturers.

Many people will be surprised that until recently, university teachers did not have to be trained in teaching methods. There is now a professional body for university teachers called Advance HE. It started as ILT (the Institute for Learning and Teaching), which became HEA (the Higher Education Academy). Academics in most universities are now expected to become Associate Fellows, often as a formal requirement of probation. Universities run qualifying courses that are approved by the body. When it started, before such courses existed, practitioners had to provide a reflective analysis of their professional work together with referees' reports. In my submission in 2000 I stated my values, and I think they still represent my views today:

- Personal respect: so I treat students as individuals.
- Relevance of motivation: so I relate to their learning contexts.
- Shared understanding: so I am explicit about tasks, roles and responsibilities.
- Lifelong learning: so I encourage learners to become increasingly independent.
- Feedback leads to improvement: so I give detailed generic and specific comments.
- Collaboration enhances product and process: so I encourage cooperation and synergy between students and colleagues.

We ran a few workshops in Dundee and some years later began the course for new lecturers, now the Postgraduate Certificate in Academic Practice in Higher Education.

Post Graduate Certificate in Academic Practice in Higher Education

The British universities eventually realised that lecturers needed to be qualified in how to teach their subject. They needed to know about learning in adults, about providing motivation and support as well as assessing students, and evaluating their own practice. I was involved in the programme for new lecturers (PGCAPHE) at Dundee University before we even merged. It was validated by the Higher Education Academy and was based on their UK Professional Standards Framework for teaching and supporting learning in higher education.

Areas of Activity
A1: Design and plan learning activities and/or programmes of study
A2: Teach and/or support learning
A3: Assess and give feedback to learners
A4: Develop effective learning environments and approaches to student support and guidance
A5: Engage in continuing professional development in subjects/disciplines and their pedagogy, incorporating research, scholarship and the evaluation of professional practices

Core Knowledge
K1: The subject material
K2: Appropriate methods for teaching and learning in the subject area and at the level of the academic programme
K3: How students learn, both generally and within their subject/disciplinary area(s)
K4: The use and value of appropriate learning technologies
K5: Methods for evaluating the effectiveness of teaching

K6: The implications of quality assurance and quality enhancement for academic and professional practice with a particular focus on teaching

Professional Values

V1: Respect individual learners and diverse learning communities

V2: Promote participation in higher education and equality of opportunity for learners

V3: Use evidence-informed approaches and the outcomes from research, scholarship and continuing professional development

V4: Acknowledge the wider context in which higher education operates recognising the implications for professional practice

This framework was useful as a planning tool and as a checklist for participants, although it is stated in very general terms. We ran an induction workshop and one activity was a card sort which stimulated discussion about their personal philosophy of teaching and learning. In small groups, the participants were asked to say whether they agreed or disagreed with the statement on each card. There were no correct answers, but the debates were spirited and thought-provoking – especially when the lecturers were from different disciplines.

Personal philosophy cards

1. I give each student the same amount of help.
2. I learn a lot from my students.
3. Creativity can be as important as certainty.
4. I teach about knowledge not general skills.

5. Cutting the failure rate is the best measure of success.
6. Regardless of their first language, students must use correct English.
7. It is not my place to provide pastoral support.
8. Lecturing may not be teaching; listening may not be learning.
9. The less I teach, the more they learn.
10. Keeping student attendance is a waste of time.
11. Student activity in a lecture is a dangerous thing to try.
12. Putting teaching materials online is just spoon-feeding students.

We also asked each person to write a specific personal concern about teaching in HE on a Post-It note. We collected them in and clustered them into themes, then asked them to work in small groups suggesting how to tackle the issues. This activity had several purposes:

- It allowed them to share their anxieties and realise that many were common worries.
- It showed them that they already knew many ways to deal with issues and thus built their confidence.
- It gave us the opportunity to talk about our own experiences.

Here are some of the issues that came up every year, along with some suggestions:

What do I do if ...?

- **...the students ask me things I do not know?**

  Be honest. Say you do not know the answers. Do not feel guilty or feel you should know everything. You could discuss methods of finding the answers and ask the students to find out and report back. Discuss possible sources to access the information required.

- **...the students treat me as a friend, joking inappropriately?**

  Establish clear boundaries. Respond calmly but firmly. Look at guidelines for professional conduct in different disciplines.

- **...some students are rude to a member of an ethnic minority community?**

  Challenge the behaviour. Spend time considering the Equality Act. Make sure you engage all students equally and fairly, modelling best practice. Consider who you will report to if this inappropriate behaviour continues.

- **...I run out of time in my lecture and have only covered half the content?**

  Make sure you and your students know which are the most important aspects. Cover them and discuss less crucial material if there is time. Be well prepared but be flexible. Consider posting additional material online.

- **...a student is upset by a low grade on their assignment?**
  Discuss the assessment criteria in detail. Explain how the student can improve. Share examples of good work.

- **...I do not know if they have understood my lecture?**
  Build in activities so they can apply the knowledge. Give them a quiz.

Each participant had a tutor from the programme team and a mentor from their own discipline. We wrote structured learning packages and had regular workshops. One module was about action research, and the new lecturers had to try out and evaluate a specific aspect of their teaching. Each person then presented their findings and reflections to the rest of the class. All members asked questions and gave detailed written comments. The final written assignment had to include a response to the issues raised by their peers.

One activity was about different modes of tutoring: face-to-face, by telephone, by letter and by email, and a colleague and I also ran it as a workshop at an international confer-

Small group work with PGCAPHE new lecturers.

ence in Dublin in 2002. Lorraine and I explored the complex role of the tutor, giving detailed constructive feedback and also listening to problems and building a relationship. We asked participants to analyse a sample letter to a distance learner and identify whether each paragraph was about the content of the student's work, giving support, motivation or interpersonal communication.

Sample Letter to a Distance Learner

Dear Jo,

Thanks for your letter and I was delighted to hear you had such a good holiday in Iceland. I went there last year and really enjoyed it.

I am pleased you sent me a draft of your assignment for some formative comments before you submit. I can see you have put a lot of work into this but it does need some changes to meet the assessment requirements.

It is essential here and in all your work to use and cite references properly. Look at how it is done in books and journals and refer to the notes and examples in the course handbook.

You need to give more detail and be more analytical in your comments. In particular:

- Page 4: relate the model to your project and explain your rationale.
- Page 6: give more detail on how the observations were conducted.

- Page 9: there is a basic flaw in your calculations. Have another look and contact me if you cannot sort it out.

You have made a good start but you need to make sure you meet criteria 3 and 5, so you will need to do some rewriting. I realise this may seem a bit demoralising, so I want to reassure you that you really are making good progress. Compared to last term, your style is clearer and you are now integrating different parts of the course.

I hope my comments are helpful. If you wish to discuss any of my points, please phone and we can talk them through. I look forward to seeing the revised final assignment by the end of the month.

I hope you enjoy the conference next week – the workshops look great.

Best wishes,
Sam

We created some scenarios and asked people to role play the tutor and the student using different modes of tutoring: face-to-face, back-to-back (to simulate a telephone discussion), and emails which they exchanged.

Scenario 1

Pat is a middle manager in a company. The current assignment is to analyse the implications of new legislation for the company (4,000 words). Pat has sent in a draft assignment. It is well written but is 6,000 words long. It only refers to Pat's own section so it is narrow in focus and does not meet the assignment requirements. Pat says writing it was useful and tells you the company wishes to use it as a starter paper.

Scenario 2

At the end of last year, due to family problems, Ali had to take some time out, but has now returned. Ali has sent you a draft, two months before final submission date. It is too short, does not focus on the task and has a very limited level of analysis. It is well below the standard required. Ali's earlier work was much better, but this seems to indicate a loss of motivation and attention.

In the plenary session we discussed the different approaches and shared what had helped or hindered the communication. We created a list of key tutor behaviours to provide effective support for their students. The workshop was lively and was voted one of the most successful at the conference.

While we were in Dublin we took the chance for a little sightseeing. It is a lovely and vibrant city with great shops, friendly people and intimidating traffic. We visited the beautiful library at Trinity College with its vaulted wooden ceiling, and marvelled over the illustrated Book of Kells. We took a city tour in an open-topped bus and were entertained by the guide, who even serenaded us with the classic song about "poor Molly Malone".

The PGCAPHE programme was evolved over the years by reducing the number of live workshops and increasing the online delivery using the VLE. Tutor support and observation of teaching remained as key features of the programme. I was always grateful for the opportunity to see so many different examples of teaching. I observed large lectures, small seminars, one-to-one supervision, practical classes and online courses. I covered subjects from engineering, nursing and international law to local history, urban geography and textile design. New lecturers on probation have a tough time. They often have to teach topics that are new to them and they must focus on research – getting funding and writing papers. So they feel very pressurised. For many, they need to get used to a new city and often a new country. Some lecturers who were initially reluctant to spend time away from their research move from angry stomping to enlightened dancing as they reflect on what they have learned about effective teaching.

The teaching observations were followed by a learning conversation in which the tutor would first ask the lecturer for a self-evaluation before discussing aspects of the performance. This was often about asking why they thought certain things had happened and what they might do differently in the future. Many of the sessions I observed were excellent, but there were also common issues. Sometimes they were technical – the lecturer could not be heard at the back, or the slides were too crowded to be legible. Often the lecturer would ask an open question and seem surprised when nobody responded. I would suggest that they set a specific question and get the students to discuss it in pairs or small groups before asking for a response. That way the students have more time to think and are offering a group response rather than opening themselves up to possible individual embarrassment. This can really help in a class of mixed ability and background.

Some of the problems could be avoided with a clearer induction so that students understood their responsibilities. Explain that they are expected to speak in class, but that the lecturer will never mind an obvious question. Breaking up a lecture with short activities and quizzes is good practice anyway. Tell the students to regard the lecture or seminar as the "filling" in the sandwich, and they must also deal with the "bread". They should come to the lecture fully prepared, having done any pre-reading, and they should follow it up by reviewing their learning and completing any given tasks. This raises another issue about when to issue PowerPoints and other materials. Some say if you give out the slides, the students will not bother to attend and so some lecturers give out incomplete PowerPoints that they complete during the lecture. Others expect students to study handouts in advance and come ready to engage with a debate. Clear guidelines and expectations can go a long way towards creating a supportive learning environment.

Students on a module may include those for whom it is a major topic for their degree, so they are likely to be motivated and interested, but others may have picked an elective almost at random and simply want to pass it. Having both groups in the same class is a challenge, but using a range of examples, and encouraging them to work in groups, where the more knowledgeable can support the weaker ones, can help.

In a large lecture theatre, some students will always sit at the back with rows of empty seats between them and the lecturer. Sometimes they do this so they can do other things, such as online shopping or checking social media on their laptops. Partly this is due to the requirement to sign in, even though physical presence is no guarantee of engagement. Overseas students may be required to attend due to visa regulations, and some professions require a minimum attendance before students are allowed out on placement.

One of the questions I always asked in my learning conversation was about how they knew what the students had understood and learned. Without some kind of test or interaction they often had no idea. Planning and delivering a well-structured lecture is fine, but teaching does not always translate into learning.

I observed a supervisor holding a regular review meeting with one of her PhD students. The lecturer was very good, asking the student to justify decisions, to consider possible interpretations and to think about the next steps in his research. She gently guided the student through a self-evaluation process, so he had to clarify his thinking. The supervisor offered encouragement and occasional suggestions for literature, but ensured the student felt empowered. The topic of the doctorate was oral cancer and the student showed a short video of cancer cells crawling past other tissues like menacing amoebae. I have never seen anything so sinister, but it explained how cancer can spread around the body so easily.

One of the strangest observations was a practical class on the physiology of the human kidney. Fifty students were split into small groups and in each group one person had to drink a large amount of water, another had to drink a strong salt solution and another did not drink at all. At intervals over a period of two hours each student produced a urine sample. The salt content was measured by a machine and the results put onto a graph. Three students did not drink anything but had to lie down in other room.

The lecturer explained that he was merely repeating the workshop that had been run this way for years, but I said I had several concerns about this:

- The measurements using the machine to measure the salt content were carried out by lab technicians, so the students did not learn how to operate the machine which might have been a useful skill.
- The three students who rested in another room did not take any part in the class so had no opportunity to learn anything.
- Some of the students who drank the salt solution reported feeling sick.
- It was a mixed class with students from many cultures and I suspect some people were uncomfortable with all the public handling of urine. There were comments about the varying shades of yellow and the lab became quite smelly.
- There was a lot of time-wasting, and the students did not seem to learn any skills or knowledge.

I suggested that the lecturer should ask his manager (who had arranged the class) about these issues, supported by the rather negative student views of the whole experience. We then discussed if there were any other ways that the students could have learned about kidney function. He said that the students could have simply been given the data from samples from previous years and discussed them.

Only on a few occasions did a lecturer fail the observation and have to repeat it. Usually it was enough to suggest a few improvements and they would normally put them into practice for their second observation. But sometimes it was not acceptable:

- One lecturer gave a brief input and dismissed the class after twenty minutes. This was not long enough for us to observe them in action, and it was not fair to shorten a lecture by so much. At the very least they could have given the class some activities to complete on their own. Sometimes you run out of content before the end of a session, so it helps to have some extra backup material with you.

- A politics lecturer spent the whole seminar explaining his own political views as if they were the only the only possible way. This was close to indoctrination of an impressionable first year class. He said he had got carried away by his own passion, but he agreed it was inappropriate so he arranged for two colleagues to present different perspectives and then asked the students to compare all three approaches.

- I observed an economics lecture talking about mathematical models in which the lecturer was unaware of the confusion in the students. She assumed (incorrectly) that they had covered some basic material already. They did not understand what she was talking about, muttered amongst themselves, and were unable to answer any of the questions she threw out to the class. After nearly half an hour, she became angry and yelled at them, and one student eventually admitted that they did not know the underpinning theory. She did then explain it, but there was no time left to cover the applications. Of course she should have been more aware of the students' lack of engagement, and she should have checked about their prior knowledge. But I felt some sympathy for her. Course leaders need to ensure their staff understand the context of what they are teaching, including any prerequisite knowledge. Students need to be told at induction that they have certain responsibilities, and they should be encouraged to speak up in such a situation. Asking questions should be seen as a strength, not a weakness.

Learning and Teaching in Higher Education

We also offered a course which became a requirement for postgraduate tutors and PhD students. These tutors often have a significant role in giving lectures and seminars, as well as marking assignments and exams. They were always keen to learn about aspects of teaching and learning, and I loved working with them. The course was five workshops plus one observation of their teaching, but they did not have to do any written assignments. The workshops were lively affairs, with two or three facilitators providing input and activities for about two dozen postgrad tutors. We modelled different ways of teaching, and for each method we gave a rationale and discussed the possible challenges:

Item	Rationale	Risk
Introductions	Establish tone	Takes time, shyness
Icebreaker	Safe discussion	May seem trivial
PowerPoint input	Key ideas, follow up	Can be a turn off
Group activities	Sharing, motivating	Take time, need variety
Oral report back	Quick	No record
Pair discussion	Deeper, more personal	Pairs may not get on

Plane evaluation	Anonymous views	May seem trivial
What next	Follow up plans	May not follow though

In the plane evaluation I ask people to write down one item on a piece of paper. It might be something they learned, or something they plan to do, or what they enjoyed most about the session. Then they make the piece of paper into a paper plane and launch it into the middle of the room. Everyone picks up a plane and reads out the comment. This gives a quick, anonymous snapshot of their opinions. Most people find it fun.

Two activities that can be effective are role-play and icebreakers, but it is best not to identify them by those names as that seems to frighten participants. I use icebreakers which relate to the topic of the course. One example is asking small groups to identify the most important skills and attitudes for teaching in HE. This is relevant, and also lets people begin to share ideas. Some icebreakers involve physical contact, which can make some people uncomfortable and may be culturally inappropriate. However, some subjects such as nursing and drama require students to touch strangers. I remember an icebreaker called "car wash" from another course. The participants form two lines to represent the brushes of a car wash, and each person in turn plays a car getting scrubbed. It did not bother me, but I cringed as a nun submitted to this experience. I wish I had been brave enough to ask the leader to choose a different activity.

We examined the pastoral aspects of the tutor role. Often they were the best people to notice if a student's behaviour suddenly changed because they were struggling. We explained the range of help and support that was available across the university, and asked them to discuss what they would do in certain scenarios. It is easy to set up guidelines about boundaries and parity of treatment, but when dealing with a specific case, sometimes human values take over. Some of the standard advice is to protect staff and students from situations that might be misinterpreted:

Would you lend money to a student?
YES/MAYBE/NO

Normally this would not be a good idea, but if the student's grant has not come through I would give them enough money for food or travel.

Would you make allowances for non-native speakers?
YES/MAYBE/NO

I am so impressed by how many students chose to study in a language which is not their native language. The university does provide extra tuition and support for such students. But should they be treated more leniently when it comes to assessing their work? It may depend on the type of course. If writing and speaking English is a key part of their module or their future profession, then they must achieve a high standard. Someone with a qualification in, say, law or education would be expected to communicate well. For other subjects, it may be more important that they can explain a concept clearly and correctly even if the language is not strictly grammatical.

Would you accept a gift from a student?
YES/MAYBE/NO

There are strict guidelines on this and a monetary limit on what can be accepted. It depends on the context. If a student brought you some sweets from their country it would seem churlish to refuse them. If student tried to give you a gift not on arrival nor on leaving but just before you marked their project, it looks suspicious.

Would you give out your personal phone number?
YES/MAYBE/NO

Now we would not normally do this, as most urgent contact is by email. But when I ran the DipEdTech I gave my students my home number. It was easier to answer a quick query on the phone, and many of them could not phone during the day as they were working.

Would you give more help to weaker students?
YES/MAYBE/NO

There is an issue here about providing the amount of help that is needed and about parity. I think that students need equal opportunity for support, but they may not all take up the offer. Some students will take advantage of a generous tutor, so it is important not to do their work for them. If I comment on a draft, I will point out the problems and correct one paragraph but expect the student to correct all the others. Also, I will explain that I will gradually reduce the amount of help to encourage independence.

Flipped learning

In the last decade we offered a full-time, campus-based Master's programme for mostly international students from China, Africa and Indonesia. The course was by blended learning: a mixture of online delivery, face-to-face workshops, individual tutorials and private study. I delivered modules on coaching, collaborative working, and inquiry methods.

I have always been keen on empowering students and involving them in taking control of their own learning, so an approach called flipped learning really appealed to me. The lecturer provides resources and activities for the students to do individually in advance of the class meeting. The group session can then engage in a deeper level of discussion. It is essential to explain the importance of preparation but, once the students accept their responsibility, it works well. For some of my Master's modules I introduced a double flip. The course was campus-based, but was largely delivered online via the VLE. The students met with me once a week for a workshop. I explained the ideas of flipped learning and we discussed the change of role of student and lecturer. I provided detailed content on the VLE, which they had to study individually before we met as a group. Then we shared ideas and I gave them a task applying the knowledge. The next week we examined how that had

Screenshot of a VLE module.

178

worked and critiqued their practice.

An approach to flipped learning

Role	VLE online	Class discussion	Home work	Class feedback
Lecturer	Design content. Add references to books, articles, videos.	Facilitate group discussion. Run workshop activities. Clarify content.	Set task. Give individual support.	Support open discussion. Give individual feedback. Generalise key ideas.
Student	Study VLE resources.	Explore and discuss. Ask questions.	Apply learning to own examples. Submit task.	Critique others' work. Amend own work.
Example: Interviews	Learn about interview process	Discuss process. Practise interviews	Design schedule. Interview each other.	Discuss experiences. Critique schedules.

This approach was popular with the students, as shown by this typical evaluative comment:

Overall I think it is an effective way of learning. Reading about the topic before the workshop gives you a chance to think about the issues and pick out some key points. The workshop discussions helped me refine my ideas and made them feel more "real" when applied to other people's examples. This gave me the confidence to tackle the homework. I appreciated having the start of the next workshop dedicated to reviewing our work and getting feedback.

I loved the interaction with the students, especially when they discussed examples from their own culture. One student worked with street children in Indonesia and had persuaded the government to issue them with birth certificates so they could begin to exist within the system. Another student talked about his village in Africa, which had been the subject of a project by the Peace Corps. They had built latrines and were surprised that only the village children used them. The project leaders had not taken the time to talk to the elders in the village, or they would have realised that the design of the buildings did not allow enough privacy and were not acceptable to the adults. This led to a fascinating discussion in the class about involving stakeholders in decision-making. Another example was about the support for orphan children with inherited AIDS which was possible in a village where everyone took some responsibility. However, similar children in the city were anonymous and subject to unhelpful legislation. I found it quite humbling to hear about these real-life cases, and to know that the skills the students learned in Dundee could have a real impact thousands of miles away.

Employability

My husband started his own business in 1992 running a garage for car repairs and servicing. He was invited to a number of practical seminars run by the local council, and I went along to support him. They covered everything from marketing and promotion to book-keeping and employment legislation. Cleverly, they covered the general principles but allowed time and individual support for us to apply them to our own circumstances. I was even able to transfer some of the aspects about management, communication and dealing with people to my own work. Key areas included how to maintain motivation, and the importance of networking and building good relationships with customers and suppliers.

They also organised three seminars by Watt Nicoll, a well-known folk singer and motivational speaker. Watt was hired by football manager Kevin Keegan to motivate the English side. He was entertaining and generous, and gave us all a copy of his book *Twisted Knickers and Stolen Scones* which contains lots of useful workshop activities that I have adapted and used many times on topics such as goal setting, time management and work/life balance.

My husband had maintained the vehicles for a local butcher, who offered Andy some strip lights when he refitted his shop. Andy's garage was rather dark, so he welcomed the offer and brought the lights home. They were covered in splashes of blood from the butchery, so we spent several hours cleaning them thoroughly before having to disinfect our kitchen. An unusual example of collaborative networking.

I was always keen that academic studies should have a real-life application, so I was delighted to be involved in a project to increase the employability of courses across the university. It soon became apparent that this was largely about changing the attitudes of both staff and students. Some academics admitted to me that they modified the learning outcomes of their modules so that they related to real-life situations, and students could see how that might be useful in future careers. They also said that they had to "hide" this from their superiors. Some lecturers seemed to think that linking to the world of work in some way devalued pure learning. I disagree, and most students do want to have a successful career. Vocational subjects such as law, nursing, engineering, or teaching indicate a clear profession. This is less obvious in the humanities, but staff can ensure that the skills and methods they teach can be transferable. The trick is to ensure that students realise that planning, investigation, analysing data and communication skills are key attributes that should appear in a job application. I applauded the architecture course that had groups of students present their design to a mock consortium of argumentative stakeholders, and then troubleshoot to provide possible solutions to issues that had arisen during construction.

We designed an audit tool and developed case studies as part of a funded project from the Scottish Higher Education Employability Network. I ran workshops across the university, and the materials were shared across the sector. This was a real example of a community of practice. We identified employability skills and attitudes, and evaluated how well professionalism and employability were integrated into curricula. The tool then encouraged staff to create an action plan to improve any areas that had a low score.

I was impressed that many students were keen to develop key skills and provide evidence of them to potential employers. Many professions and vocations are regulated by a professional statutory body which validates academic programmes and monitors workers. Some list a range of competences which must be achieved alongside academic assessments, and curriculum designers must relate to both practical professional requirements as well as intellectual qualities.

The Quality Assurance Agency, Scotland is involved in development and quality enhancement activities to reflect the needs of HE, and I have been part of several of their initiatives. One QAA project was on work-based learning (WBL). With Ian Ball, I designed "Making it work: a guidebook exploring work-based learning", a detailed resource for managers in industry and tutors in Higher Education Institutions (HEIs). It is available as a hard-copy and also as a website, and was launched at a series of workshops. It includes case studies, links to literature and analytical tools. The focus was on supporting systems that allow employee-students to integrate learning and practice in order to gain qualifications. It can be a valuable approach to develop the workforce without interrupting their paid work. Two of the most important areas are support for and assessment of the employee-students. This is an excerpt:

> WBL provides the reality of an authentic context for learning which also produces the currency of transferable credit. It helps to set up a learning agreement related to the specific needs of each student. A three-way agreement between the student, the HEI tutor and the workplace tutor can work really well. This can aid planning, resourcing, monitoring and review. Assessment is useful to measure learning for certification and to monitor progress. It needs to be realistic and relevant

for all stakeholders and it is termed authentic assessment. Students must find it challenging and satisfying; employers must find it relevant to their work context; HEIs must find it provides evidence of achievement at an appropriate level. The roles and responsibilities of each stakeholder must be clear. It is essential that the student does not receive conflicting advice from different supporters. Effective collaborations depend on time and commitment and a sharing of values.

An effective curriculum needs to be aligned in two different ways. The learning outcomes, teaching methods and assessment must mesh together; you cannot test a practical objective by a written assignment alone. Also, new learning needs to be scaffolded onto existing knowledge and frameworks; tutors must encourage students to see the links and to apply ideas to their own context.

I worked on another QAA project with Ian Ball: "A toolkit for enhancing personal development planning strategy, policy and practice in higher education institutions." Personal development planning (PDP) provides a framework for organising and recording WBL and Placement Learning (PL) experiences, as explained here:

> The value of PDP in WBL is significant as it can be the single place where the employee-student can collate and synthesise all their learning experiences. It can become:
> - A repository for evidence of competence.
> - The mechanism for recording personal and professional thoughts, feelings and reflective accounts.

- The place where mapping of knowledge, skills and experiences against career aspirations is located.
- A vehicle for assessment.

PDP is valuable in stimulating reflection in PL before and after placement. As it is so personal and individual it is more likely to lead to deep learning. A major aspect of PL is the social and cultural context. The learner must fit in with local traditions, work as part of a team and contribute to a community of practice. These soft skills are important for employability and relevant learning outcomes can be incorporated into PDP. This is normally by the student's initial self-assessment followed by witness statements accompanied by a reflective account from the learner.

Many universities (but not yet Dundee) have identified a range of generic skills which they label "graduate attributes" and represent the qualities an employer could reasonably expect from a first degree. The idea of personal development planning is to let students develop and showcase such skills.

Staff Development Projects

The Children's Panel system in Scotland combined justice and welfare for children and young people, aiming to deal with their "deeds and needs". I worked as a consultant, helping them to redesign a core curriculum for officers and volunteers, providing workshops on assertiveness for members, and creating a training package for the Children's Panel Advisory

Committee (CPAC Matters). This was a national initiative funded by the Scottish Office and supported by discussions with children's panels across the country. The Deputy Minister for Children and Education wrote the foreword, and there was a big launch event in Edinburgh in 2000.

The advisory committee was concerned with recruiting and monitoring the panel members. As part of the preparation, I was allowed to observe some sessions of a children's panel. I do hope that my experiences were not typical. I was amazed that no account seemed to be taken of values when appointing members. Some of the people that I watched making decisions affecting the lives of children and their families demonstrated racist and patronising attitudes, with little sign of compassion or empathy for those involved.

We designed a training package of interactive tasks using workbooks and videos. The design team of five academics included myself and three of my previous students, two of them working in other universities. We drafted outline scripts, but left the detail to the actors to improvise. We used real panel members, staff from the drama department of the college and children from a local school. We shot several scenarios and put them onto a CD-ROM. They could be studied in order, or related aspects could be viewed together. We followed three panel members through recruitment and monitoring while they attended panels dealing with children who were involved in crime or in need of protection. Another scenario investigated a complaint against a panel member.

The subject was emotive and the actors were impressive. One lady in particular inspired me. She had been a panel member for many years, and used her experience to add authenticity. After a long day of filming she seemed very tired, and explained she had terminal cancer but was committed to being part of this very important project. She died a few weeks later, and I was pleased to be able to give her husband a video compilation of her role. I already knew him, as he was an FE lecturer and was a member of the Grampian Open Learning Association.

It was a complex project, both technically and political-ly. We had to create materials that would suit all the different local authorities in Scotland, each with their own subtle varia-tion of procedure. One of the characters was called Claire, but West coast members insisted we change the spelling to "Clare". However, it is one of the products from my long ca-reer of which I am most proud. The systems have changed, but it still has valuable lessons about how to conduct inter-views, listen to opinions and share ideas. It still looks smart and stylish with its purple and turquoise livery.

I was involved in lots of inter-institutional projects, and always enjoyed the networking as well as the tasks. One of my favourites was the creation of the Evaluation Cookbook. This is a book of 88 pages with recipes for methods of evalua-tion written in a simple and accessible way. Students (and staff) found it was a very practical introduction to useful techniques. It was funded by the Scottish Higher Education Funding Council (SHEFC), and was led by a project based at Heriot-Watt University. The 25 contributors communicated by a private website, a mailbase discussion group and email. I wrote one of my chapters with a colleague from Hull, but we never met. The only time that most of the authors came to-gether was for the official launch in Edinburgh. One of the recipes was for chocolate cake to be used as a reward or a cel-ebration, and that was certainly a feature of the launch; it was delicious. The book was useful as a hard-copy, but it was also made available online through a web provider. The danger was that when the provider ceased to exist, the resources would be lost. Fortunately another provider took on the responsibility. I was horrified to see that the book is available on Amazon at a high price. This seems reprehensible when the resource was free and we were all happy to be involved for no financial reward.

Another SHEFC-funded initiative involved a dozen related projects on effective teaching using technology. I was the leader of a project in North-East Scotland with colleagues from Northern College, the University of Dundee, the University of Aberdeen and the University of the Highlands and Islands (Perth). We held monthly meetings alternating face-to-face sessions, which included a tasty lunch, with video conferences. In those days, holding a video conference meant booking your institution's video conference suite and allowing for differences in bandwidth, which slowed down the communication. Now we can link up via personal laptops or phones and exchange documents at the same time.

We developed a useful resource called ToolCIT which collated audit tools, action tools and advice tools for effective teaching and learning. It contained a series of activities that could be done by individuals or teams, as well as links to a selected range of online exemplar resources. We made this available on a website, but were concerned about what would happen when the project ended so we asked for additional funding to create CD-ROMs. These discs were issued to each institution, and they contained all the links to the relevant web resources. It was a very enjoyable project, except that I had to produce a monthly report of progress and finance. This was tedious and seemed to be overkill for a grant that was very small, and the only expenses were travel and subsistence.

We met with the other projects and carried out some joint reviews of each other's developments. An external evaluator was brought in, and I provided her with all of our minutes and reports. I was appalled to see a discussion of ToolCIT in the project newsletter appearing under both our names. I had not seen, let alone approved, the copy and it made no mention of any other colleagues involved in the project. I immediately contacted the coordinator and insisted that the item was removed from the newsletter. Fortunately it was only distributed electronically and it was changed at once. I also contacted my team members to explain what had happened and to ensure them that any article would be published on behalf of us all and only after consultation. The coordination between the different projects was not well managed. It gobbled up a lot of the available money, and did not give us support when it was needed.

Our resource was well-received, and evaluation showed that people found it useful, easy to navigate and attractive. Interviews of the team members suggested they had learned a great deal and had enjoyed the cross-institutional collaboration. I was gratified that they praised my "excellent management... whilst she was at time a hard task-master, this was done in such a deft way that the team did not realise they had been managed so well until the task was completed."

Another Dundee/Aberdeen collaboration funded by a European initiative was to create some web-based training materials for SMEs (Small to Medium Sized Enterprises). This was part of a "just-in-time" initiative, aimed largely at the offshore oil and gas industries. Our topics were effective learning and mentoring, two subjects I have taught in many ways from live workshops to online modules. One of the most interesting aspects was the developmental testing when I watched a participant working through my materials. It was fascinating to note which route they took, how they responded to the questions and activities. They filled in a questionnaire at the end, but also engaged in a useful dialogue explaining what they were thinking when they made certain choices. Their comments allowed me to enhance the structure, add extra items and improve the navigation.

Croatia

Flexible Learning Interactive (FLI) is an online resource for staff that I developed with one of the university's learning technologists. We introduced the ideas of flexibilities within different aspects of the curriculum and gave advice and examples on how to develop modules in a virtual learning environment.

A group of academic staff developers from the Balkan countries visited the university, and I was asked to talk about my FLI resource. My presentation and demonstration only lasted about forty minutes, but the visitors seemed very impressed. One professor from Croatia gave me her business card and said she would be in touch. I did not think any more about it until I got an email from her several months later. She had secured funding and invited me to repeat my session for her colleagues at the University of Zagreb. I agreed, but said that if I were going all that way, would she like me to run staff development workshops on other topics such as evaluation, assessment or mentoring? She put together a three-day programme, and I headed to Zagreb in November 2008.

I ran practical workshops for staff on methods they could apply immediately to their teaching. I also had a couple of meetings with senior staff discussing our educational systems. Some of our fundamental concepts such as learning outcomes, student autonomy and formative assessment seemed alien to the lecturers I met, which of course was the reason I had been invited. These discussions would affect the underlying educational philosophy across the university sector in Croatia. They had a few bursaries to award to students, and they were given to those who scored highest in exams. I did wonder if they should have given the funds to weaker students who perhaps had greater need of financial support.

Many of the participants in my workshops did not speak good English, so I spoke slowly and used a lot of visual aids. I left my PowerPoint slides and online learning modules with them to study at their leisure. For my main presentation about flexible learning to a large audience, they set up a video camera. I assumed this was to record my session for future use and was rather bemused that they streamed it over the internet without even asking me.

The staff were very kind to me and gave me "pocket money" for incidental expenses as well as paying my travel costs. They took me out to dinner every night, gave me a beautiful silk scarf with the university crest on it and put me up in a luxury hotel. I had a spare half-day to explore, so I went to the top of the old city on the funicular rail-

One of my presentations in Zagreb.

way and walked back down enjoying a delicious pastry in a café on the way. This is a personal account I wrote about my trip:

Zagreb has an old-world charm of opulent and ornate buildings, and frequent squares with statues and red umbrellas over market stalls. The harsh sun bleaches the buildings leaving them sterilised against an azure sky. The cathedral with its twin spires of lofty filigree, decorative carving and shafting stained glass seems sanitised rather than sacred.

The language is strange as it has too many consonants and too few vowels. Some words have as many as five consonants together, those which would not normally sit next to each other in English such as blj, ml, jj, dstv. The computer keyboard is different with the "z" very prominent. Then sometimes the vowels want to make their presence felt so you get three letter "u"s together. The writing looks like a text message or a personal ad. After a few hours I found I was mimicking their speech patterns. Their English was good with an accurate vocabulary but the sentence structure was simplified with an unusual sequence. So it was not so much "pidgin English" as "English pigeon".

After the break-up of Yugoslavia, Croatia developed its own monetary system. The currency is based on the old method of trading in the skins of weasels which had been trapped by hunters. The

Croatian word for weasel is Kuna so that became the unit of currency and each coin has the animal depicted on it.

Evaluation

I was involved in some courses that ran for many years and regular evaluation, review and improvement were ongoing processes. I liked to see the impact of my work. One of the frustrations of working as a consultant or designing materials for an outside client was that I often did not know how or if my ideas had been successful. National projects were usually evaluated by another team and the results were not made public, and were sometimes reviewed with a political agenda as well as an educational one.

I ran modules and workshops on evaluation methodology and applied the processes to my own courses. I followed this model:

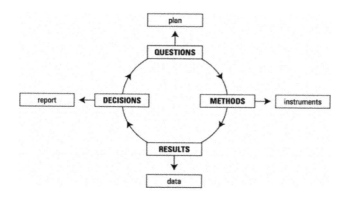

It starts with the analysis of the key questions about the context and the purposes of the evaluation and leads to the formulation of the plan. The choice of methods for the collection of data is followed by the creation of instruments. The results are presented as qualitative and quantitative data. These allow the decisions to be made and a report of the outcomes and the way forward. Then the cycle continues. All stakeholders can contribute at all stages, and are more likely to accept future changes if they have been empowered by the process.

The regular quality assurance procedures required formal evaluations, but they often focused on quantitative aspects. I was always more interested in qualitative measures of students' views about aspects of the course. I used standard methods such as questionnaires and interviews to collect views, and I also used a variety of more unusual participatory approaches. I asked students to write comments on coloured Post-It notes in the traffic lights method. Aspects they wanted the tutors to start were put on green Post-Its, things the tutors should continue went on orange ones, and things they should stop went on red Post-Its. When I displayed them on a flipchart I responded, promising to act on some issues and explaining why some wishes could not be met. I kept the flipchart up so that students could see when progress was made in response to their comments.

Chapter Seven

Retirement

When I reached 40 years of service in Dundee, my colleagues threw me a surprise party with a card, a beautiful cake, wine, flowers and gifts including a stunning necklace. When I reached the age of 65 I semi-retired, and worked only three days a week. I worked on Tuesday, Wednesday and Thursday, allowing me to have long weekends that I could enjoy with my husband in our motorhome. It suited me very well, and I had no plans to retire totally.

However when I was 74 I received an email from my pension provider talking about the investment of my lump sum. It was only when I had a meeting with our finance officer that I realised the true meaning of that ambiguous email. My pension was generous,

Cutting into my cake.

and included a lump sum plus a monthly pension. But if you wanted to work beyond the age of 75, you could not take your lump sum. Instead it was reallocated and spread across your monthly pension. I presume they hoped you would die long before you received it all, thus saving them money. So I had a stark choice: retire before my next birthday or lose my lump sum worth thousands of pounds. It did not feel like a choice but a fait accompli, so I tendered my resignation.

I was furious and upset and, in a way, grieving for my lost career. I did not feel I was ready to leave and thought that I still had a lot to offer. In the past I had sometimes suffered from the imposter syndrome, feeling unworthy of my role and worried I would be found out; enforced retirement caused the opposite reaction. I deserved a job, I had useful skills and I was a valuable asset. I felt diminished as a person. My colleagues were shocked and angry about my departure too. My department had plans for my future work commitments which had to be directed to other staff. This chronicle has reminded me how much I have achieved in my long career. I am grateful and proud, but also sad that I am no longer accountable.

I attended a workshop on preparation for retirement and we had to list the things we would miss and those we would not miss about our occupation. Here are my lists.

What will I not miss?
- Sharing a room. (Once I was part-time I had to share an office. Although I liked my considerate roommate, I missed the privacy.)
- Technology problems. (We were very dependent on the online environment for all aspects of communication, but it was not always reliable and the

systems kept changing. We had different versions of software in our offices and our teaching rooms.)
- Centralised systems and regulations. (In particular, the attempt to have a "one size fits all" approach to student learning which frequently disadvantaged part-time distance learners.)
- Research focus. (Teaching often felt like an inferior role beside research, even though in our department we made more money from teaching than research.)
- Parking and driving. (Parking had been free at Northern College and the university was expensive. You had to get in early to secure a parking place, and I hated driving through the rush hour traffic.)

What will I miss?
- Designing and delivering workshops. (I loved the buzz of face-to-face delivery, and the dynamic interaction of a group.)
- Designing modules. (I liked structuring ideas and presenting information in an engaging way using a variety of technologies.)
- Tutoring students. (I enjoyed building a supportive relationship with individual students, face-to-face or at a distance.)
- Peer mentoring. (A very positive ongoing professional and personal support system.)
- Observations of teaching. (Seeing ideas from different disciplines.)

- Working across the university. (Making connections and using transferable ideas.)
- Learning new approaches. (I have always been keen to try new things and apply them to my own situation.)
- Chatting to friends. (The informal interactions were such a positive part of my career.)

I had planned my last month carefully, wanting to enjoy my last few workshops and tutorials, and had even selected my clothes, but a little thing called Covid-19 had other ideas. My retirement and the first lockdown merged into one amorphous confusion. Suddenly there was no chance for a long motorhome trip, nor the increased visits to concerts, theatre, art galleries and museums that we had wanted.

The pandemic and the strange twilight world we were plunged into were hard to comprehend. It was a real case of lifelong or life-wide learning. I was lucky in that I did not have the problems that affected many people. I was financially secure, reasonably healthy, without any caring responsibilities and living in a comfortable home with my husband. But it was still frustrating and tedious. I managed to maintain a routine. I got up before eight, did not succumb to watching daytime TV, and maintained regular contact with friends and family. I missed my exercise class, but I walked every day, always thankful for having the River Tay just a few hundred yards away, and continued my normal meditation practice. I was grateful for online courses and for the time to focus on my writing. I felt the occasional twinge of guilt about the cupboards that were not yet decluttered, but I could not do much while charity shops and local recycling centres remained closed.

My generous colleagues showered me with gifts again. This time retirement presents were ordered online and delivered by lorries. They included wine, chocolates, flowers, cakes, cheese, electronic cards with affectionate messages, and a painting which apparently represents me. I had not realised I was so popular, but then I had tutored most of them. Here is my electronic thank you note to them:

Thank you so much for the good wishes and the wonderful retirement gifts. I have loved my career in higher education - 6 years at Glasgow University and 45 years in Dundee. I have worked with some amazing colleagues and some inspirational students. I have been involved in a wide range of projects and national initiatives and have travelled to ten countries. I will miss it.

I will follow in the footsteps of the Dundee poet William Topaz McGonagall ("the worst poet in the history of the English language") and leave you with a poem:

Pandemic

The daily death lists on the news
Give us pause for thought.
So many grieving families,
So many lives cut short.

Unemployment is set to rise.
Prosperity then ceases.
In this worldwide catastrophe
Who picks up the pieces?

Key workers are all so busy,
Stressed and inundated.
Stay-at-homes are idle, feeling
Worthless and frustrated.

Isolated from our neighbours,
Yet every Thursday night
We venture out onto the street
And clap for all our might.

The kindnesses of the strangers
Passing you in the street.
They smile with open hopefulness
Although you never meet.

With letters, emails and Skype
We contact our old friends,
And promise to maintain the links
When this hard lockdown ends.

A host of golden daffodils
Are dancing in the breeze
Oblivious to the virus.
A lovely sight to please!

Mating birds and bright spring flowers
Display their brilliance,
Encourage us to do the same -
Show our resilience.

Coaltits are nesting in the wall
And foraging for worms.
Nature carries on regardless
In no uncertain terms.

Restless waves still wash the beaches,
Constantly dynamic.
How can we try to turn the tide
On this huge pandemic?

We tend the garden, clean the house,
Watching our plans shatter.
On reflection now we know it's
Those we love who matter.

With faith and hope and charity
We'll fight austerity.
We'll strive to build a better world,
Gifting posterity.

Best wishes,
Gaye Manwaring

My Honorary Role

The university was happy to make me an honorary senior lecturer, and I did some voluntary work. I continued to support my students and mark assignments for my modules. I joined the programme board for the BAPD, and I ran several courses on student wellbeing. Due to the restrictions imposed by the pandemic, all this work was done remotely from home.

I learned a lot about running courses by Microsoft Teams and Zoom, and using quick response tools like Mentimeter which allow students to give comments anonymously. I enjoyed it, but part of me was relieved that I was not under the same pressure as my colleagues who were swamped with complex technological demands for delivering and recording teaching sessions.

I did not want to be lazy. I wanted to keep my mind active, and I wanted to feel useful. So a colleague, Jill Shimi, and I decided to occupy our first lockdown summer with a useful exercise. We contacted some newly-appointed staff and asked what had most helped them and what had most worried them when they joined the university. Based on our long experience of supporting new staff and linked to their comments, we created an interactive resource which we emailed out to all colleagues. It contains lots of useful ideas and activities as well as hotlinks to web resources. This is part of the introduction:

> The guide is mainly aimed at new university lecturers starting their career with probably a mixture of excitement, anticipation and some anxiety. We offer you a range of ideas, questions, tools and resources to help you craft your own approach to teaching in higher education. We hope to stimulate your thoughts and encourage you to apply new practices within your own context. Experimentation, evaluation and reflection are essential ongoing methods which will help you create and live your own philosophy of teaching. This resource contains our input which includes activities. Some of these are to stimulate your thoughts while others encourage you to investigate the ideas

further. Ideally you could try to implement some aspects within your practice. Your logbook is for you to record your key thoughts and learning points as you progress.

It was well-received by experienced colleagues as well as new ones. QAA (the Quality Assurance Agency for Higher Education) thought it could be adapted to be useful to students, which led to us developing an interactive resilience game. Continuing to be involved in such projects certainly developed my own resilience.

Part 3:
Learning My Living; Living My Learning

As I wrote about my academic life in chronological order, I noticed several recurring themes. They show many links between different aspects of my career, and demonstrate the value of transferability.

Chapter Eight

Reflection, Mentoring and Resilience

The above three themes have permeated my academic life. They hang together, and I have written about them all. The common threads are about empowerment and using the past and the present to improve the way you behave in the future.

- **Reflection** has been a professional requirement for me and my colleagues, and is a key part of most courses I have taught.
- I have developed and evaluated **mentoring** schemes, run training workshops on mentoring and designed modules on mentoring and coaching. It has been part of a professional support mechanism for me, both as a mentee and as a mentor.
- **Resilience** has featured as a key part in my wellbeing courses.

Reflection

There are many models of reflection, but none quite suited me so I developed my own framework. I called it the conjunction model of reflection; it considers the conjunction between different aspects of a situation, and it uses grammatical conjunctions as prompts within an analytical template. Colleagues and students have found this to be a useful way to structure their reflection, ensuring that it leads to transferable learning and improved practice.

Conjunction Framework of Reflection

WHAT: description	
What happened? Who was involved?	
WHY: analysis	
Why did you behave as you did? How did you feel? Why do you think others behaved as they did? What contextual factors were under your control? What could have been different?	
SO: specific plan	**ALSO: generalised plan**
What will you do next? Why? What outcome do you expect?	What could you have done differently? What preparation would help in future?
BUT: other considerations	**BUT: other considerations**
Do you have all the information you need? Are there other possible actions? Will it affect anyone else?	Do you need a range of strategies for different contexts?

THEN: policy
Are there bigger issues here? Who do you discuss it with?

Example:

WHAT: description	
A student complained that I had failed her assignment but her mentor had told her it was fine.	
WHY: analysis	
The student received mixed messages from me (the marker) and the mentor. This was complicated by the fact that the mentor was also the student's line manager. The mentor had taken the course some years before, but it was an earlier version of the module. There seems to be confusion about the role of the mentor which is to support the student, not to mark the work. The mentor should encourage the student to self-assess against the module criteria.	
SO: specific plan	**ALSO: generalised plan**
I need to ensure that the student understands what she has to do to resubmit the work.	I need to provide more support for mentors and ensure everyone under-stands the roles.
BUT: other considerations	**BUT: other considerations**
I will also need to rebuild my relationship with the student.	I have no quality control over mentors.
THEN: policy	
The course leader should consider training sessions for	

all mentors and giving more guidance about roles and responsibilities in the course handbook.

The concept of reflexivity is broader than reflection. It is complex and nebulous. It includes thinking about what has happened, looking at one's values and beliefs, analysing the context, and leading to considered action. I see this as four mirrors, looking backwards, inwards, outwards, and forwards. I introduce it to my students using the metaphors of a concave mirror reflecting the past, a microscope for self-analysis, a periscope for horizon scanning, and a convex mirror beaming forward.

	LOOKING OUTWARDS environment contexts constraints	
LOOKING BACKWARDS reflection experiences events conversations memories	**REFLEXIVITY**	LOOKING FORWARDS plans actions intentions practice learning
	LOOKING IN-WARDS personal values personal beliefs prejudices emotions	

Mentoring

I think that most people have a mentor even if they do not realise it. Think about the child chatting to their grandparents or seeking help from an elder sibling. Many pub regulars unload their worries to the landlord. Apprentices soon find out the best person to ask, and it often is not their line manager. Best friends are there in good times and bad. These informal mentors are good listeners, not judging nor advising, but empathising and allowing the person to come to their own decisions. This can lead to self-awareness and personal growth.

Many organisations have mentoring schemes and an important decision is how mentors and mentees are matched. If the mentor also has a managerial or assessor role, the mentee may be reluctant to share any problems in case they are seen as weaknesses. If mentees choose a friend as a formal mentor, the relationship may be too cosy. A good mentor offers challenge as well as support. In many modules, mentors are previous course members. This can be useful as they have experienced the programme, but if the assignments have changed it can be difficult. A student may get conflicting advice from a mentor and a tutor. Roles, expectations and boundaries must be clear.

It often helps if there is a separation between the two parties. Many firms have cross-mentoring programmes which works well because the problems encountered by staff are often universal and an uninvolved viewpoint can be valuable. I have organised two such systems – between the Dundee and Aberdeen campuses of Northern College, and between the Universities of Dundee and St Andrews. In both cases several people opted to have a mentor from the other place. I designed the schemes, conducted the training, participated and carried out an evaluation. I am convinced that mentoring is a powerful and effective tool for staff development and management. I am delighted that mentoring is now championed and supported by the university.

There are lots of frameworks that mentors can use, but most involve listening to help the mentee analyse the issue and then exploring different options. What do you think would happen if you did this? What might happen if you said that? What would happen if you chose to do nothing? A good mentor will help the mentee see beyond the immediate situation so it can be an opportunity for learning and improved practice. A mentoring session will normally end with a set of precise targets which can be revisited at the start of the next meeting. The GROW and CLEAR models are common frameworks to analyse an issue and plan a way forward.

G Goal	**C** Contract
R Reality	**L** Listen
O Options or obstacles	**E** Explore options and implications
W Way forward or What you Will do	**A** Action
	R Review and Reflect

Mentoring discussions need to lead to action, and it helps if the action plan is based on SMART targets rather than general ideas:

S	Specific, Sensible
M	Measurable, Motivating
A	Achievable, Agreed
R	Relevant, Realistic

T	Time bound, Timely

A small team of colleagues delivered mentoring workshops in several departments across the university, and we also ran in-service training for outside organisations who paid the university a hefty fee for our services. We ran an extensive mentoring programme in a prestigious public school. Most members of our delivery team were socialists and not in favour of private education. But we were impressed with many aspects of the school's ethos, resources and curriculum. We were invited to planning meetings (with wonderful food and wine) and ran several workshops for the staff. The headteacher bravely agreed to be mentored by one of us in front of the whole staff. The interview was powerful and explored areas of tension and possible strategies for tackling them. The staff were clearly impressed by this honest and open discussion, and it did more than all our workshop activities to persuade the teachers that the mentoring process was valuable and insightful. We linked the workshops to a distance learning module about mentoring. Staff studied the module materials online, practiced mentoring with their colleagues and wrote about their experiences in their assignments. We acted as tutors to support and assess them. It was a successful project, and many staff found the process of being a mentor or a mentee led to useful reflection about their teaching approaches, management style and career plans. One aspect that was less than ideal was that the mentor-mentee relationships were based on the standard school hierarchy so that mentees were mentored by their line manager, which sometimes inhibited the sharing of concerns.

I was recently part of a mentoring pilot run by the Royal Society of Arts for Fellows in Scotland and Australia.

Some mentees focused on a specific project while others wanted an open exploration of part of their life. Exeter University has advertised for alumni to act as career mentors to their students, so I have put my name forward. I am delighted that such a simple cost-effective process is now valued by hard-headed businesses as staff development for all involved.

Resilience

Resilience combines inner strength with the ability to deal positively with challenges and turn them into opportunities for growth. I wrote a chapter about resilience with Jill Shimi. We interviewed staff and students about the strategies they used and described many valuable approaches. This summarises our conclusions:

We have represented resilience development as a diagram which shows the process and progression from entry into higher education, through the four facets of resilience, leading to a person who is fully aware of their own potential and uses a range of strategies to function effectively in an uncertain world.

>>>>> INCREASING RESILIENCE >>>>>		
Previous experiences	Confidence	Metacognition
Personal characteristics	Adaptability	Self esteem
Current challenges	Purposefulness	Personal growth
	Social support	Professional development

We make the following recommendations:

For the institution:
- Provide coherent resilience training for staff, both for personal development and to help them support their students.
- Build resilience into the curriculum content.
- Continue to provide relevant inputs for students such as stress management.
- Continue to offer a range of coordinated student support services that are well advertised.

For the staff:
- Teach resilience as a topic and as a set of skills within courses.
- Make it explicit in learning outcomes and assessment criteria.
- Develop supportive individual relationships with students.
- Relate teaching, assessment and support to students' strengths, needs, and contexts.

For students:
- Learn about resilience as a topic.
- Develop your own resilience.
- Help your peers to become more resilient.
- Find ways to demonstrate your resilience to prospective employers.

The idea of resilience also led me to write a poem:

Hope springs ... spring hopes

Spring!
This onomatopoeic season
gives a lesson
in resilience.
We must bounce back from winter snow,
And focus on the future now.
Spring flowers bloom in sequence through
nature's orchestration.
Starlings celebrate the change
with song and murmuration.
Colours vibrant.
Birdsong urgent.
Spring!

Chapter Nine

Volunteering

I have volunteered for several different charities, but always doing something to help people directly rather than fundraising. I found there were lots of transferable skills, and I often used strategies from voluntary work in my professional situation and vice versa. I have noticed how volunteering has become more formalised, involving careful selection and training as well as monitoring and support of volunteers. I applaud this approach which protects all involved but there are times when the balance of regulation outweighs that of humanity, and I have seen more petty political infighting in the voluntary sector than in education. I have also seen situations where volunteers were treated badly by paid professionals. The volunteers felt resented and were made to feel like second class citizens, which undermined their confidence. One of my doctoral students investigated the role of volunteers in hospices and proposed various ways that the organisations could improve the way they supported this valuable human resource.

A fellow student at Exeter had severe mental health problems and she was eventually committed to a local mental hospital. I used to visit her and was invited to a dance there. I enjoyed waltzing with one inmate who was a traditional tall, dark handsome stranger and I was amazed when a staff member told me, inappropriately, that he was a convicted psychopathic murderer.

With CRUSE, the bereavement charity, the training was done in the psychiatry department at Ninewells Hospital in Dundee and it was my introduction to a counselling style of listening which I subsequently used when tutoring students and mentoring colleagues. Over the next few years I met many grieving people, and I think I helped them cope with their loss. Often a small action signalled the beginning of healing. One woman would never use the chair that her been her father's, even though it had the best position in the lounge. One day, she just sat down in it and smiled – it had become just an armchair, not an absent parent.

I remember a young bereaved woman whom I visited for fifteen months until she felt ready to stop the meetings. In all that time she had been given just two meetings of five minutes with a mental health professional. For the first three months we just talked. Then for a few weeks she made me a cup of tea, and eventually made one for herself as well, although she did not drink it. At the end of a year she made us both tea and she drank hers as well.

One lady was grieving for her adult daughter, her only child, who had been killed in a road accident. She kept herself busy knitting clothes for the grandchildren she would now never have. Eventually she was able to start knitting items for living family members, and she bravely gave all the baby clothes to a charity.

I visited one lady in the middle of the day and she made me a pile of sandwiches, even though I had had my own lunch before I arrived. I explained that I did not want her to give me lunch, but it was her way of thanking me. I changed the meetings to the morning, on my way to work. But she presented me with a delicious bacon roll. It is hard to adopt the appropriate listening stance with butter on your chin!

Often people said grief made them behave irrationally. An elderly widower said he could only sleep when he cuddled his dead wife's nightie. One lady was in floods of tears when cleaning the gutter. She was well able to do the task, but it had been something her late husband had always done and the action just brought home her loss. A man who broke his wrist said he could cope with losing his wife or with a broken bone, but not both issues at the same time. I sympathised, as I remember throwing away a plant that a friend had given me because I was so angry the plant was thriving while my friend was dead. For months after my father died I purchased books I knew he would have liked and they are still unread, but owning them somehow made a connection.

Victim Support was linked with the local police force and – bizarrely – as you became more experienced you progressed to more serious crimes, so if you were successful with burglary you moved up to assault. Time and again I was struck by the impact that even minor crime could have on people's confidence, ridding them of the ability to go out or to feel comfortable in their own home. Theft was more about a sense of violation than about the loss of what was stolen. A personal attack sometimes made the victim feel as if they deserved it and led to low self-esteem.

The training course was powerful and thought-provoking. I remember one exercise where we were each allocated a persona such as single mother, drug addict, partially sighted person, indicating aspects of their home background, age, education, employment and so on. Then we were given different scenarios such as accepting a college place, buying a new car or going on holiday and asked to step forward if we felt our persona would be likely or able to do so. I felt a real sense of injustice as I saw other trainees moving forward and taking opportunities that seemed beyond my reach.

I trained as an audio describer at Perth Rep and later used my skills at Dundee Rep as well. We provided an audio description to visually impaired members of the audience. We watched the stage with closed circuit TV and gave our commentary into a microphone. They sat in the auditorium and wore headphones. We worked in teams of three. One person described the set and costumes and the other two described the action in alternate scenes. The skill was to time your words in between the actors' speech so you did not speak over them. We had a copy of the script which was fine until the actors improvised. I loved doing it and enjoyed getting a deeper insight into the plays. For instance, I noticed that a villain coming down the stairs towards a victim was much more menacing than if he had been walking across the room. Sometimes you need to alert the audience to future events. If the murderer was going to hide the gun in the coal scuttle you need to make sure you mentioned this part of the set. In preparation we had to watch the play several times. We were asked to make notes on our script using a small pen torch. Once we explained what we were doing, the nearby members of the audience were fine. But the actors did not really like it and complained they found the small lights in the auditorium distracting. Years earlier they would have had most of the audience lighting cigarettes. I presume they felt the same way about having signers at the side of the stage for patrons who were hard of hearing. I found their attitude annoying. We were giving our time for free to help them reach a wider audience.

I volunteered with a local organisation called Advocating Together, supporting adults with learning disabilities and autism. We ran workshops to encourage participation, build confidence and improve communication skills. When Dundee was competing to become the City of Culture (we came second), I asked them to identify the key aspects of the city and vote on the most important. The River Tay was a clear favourite. We spent several weeks drawing pictures to represent the city, and the posters were displayed at an event organised by the university. I learned to adapt activities to an audience with low levels of literacy and numeracy, and I developed the ability to talk with the participants without being patronising or superior.

The focus was all about empowerment. I was impressed by the resilience of the members as they struggled and

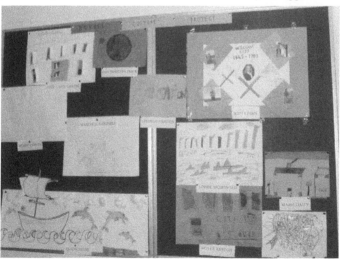

Advocating Together collage about Dundee.

coped with normal life challenges linked to employment, life-style and relationships alongside their disabilities. When I left, we all went out for a meal and I wrote them a little poem which they insisted I recite several times:

> Children need a mum and dad
> To give the help and love they had.
> Adults a want to air their voices,
> Spread their wings, make their own choices.
> Mutual aid works in any weather
> So please support "Advocating Together".

Chapter Ten

Wellbeing

In 2007 I was diagnosed with a serious chronic illness that has hospitalised me three times (so far) and has had a major impact on my life. I saw an advert in the local library for a free course on self-management for those with a chronic health condition. It was run by Arthritis Care and was for any illness so I enrolled. It was limited to twelve participants, and over six weeks we dealt with our attitudes to our conditions and developed action plans for a better life. I soon realised that the content was fairly basic, but the interaction and mutual support from the group was crucial. I applied to become a trainer and, with a partner, ran a lot of courses over a period of several years.

My partner, Elisabeth Hill, was a remarkable lady. She had enjoyed many experiences and jobs in a varied career, but she had never studied at university. She enrolled on the BAPD programme and completed a diploma and was the oldest person at graduation aged 82. She really enjoyed the on-campus workshops and became a class rep. Her assignments were full of reflection and detailed examples from her practice. I watched her abilities in academic work grow and I loved this comment she made: "I have the confidence to pass and the self-confidence to fail". She knew she would be able to access and use the support from tutors if she had to resubmit an assignment.

Exemplar certificate for course participants

We covered basic topics in the self-management course such as stress, relaxation, diet, exercise and communication. I developed some lively activities and useful visuals using PowerPoint slides, but again the keys were mutual support and helping people take charge of their life by managing their condition. At the end of the course we encouraged the group to continue meeting regularly, and many did so.

Arthritis Care gave each person an attendance certificate listing which sessions they had attended. We felt this had a rather negative impact, as several people missed one of the workshops due to a flare up or a medical appointment. So we created a scroll which they really liked.

Participants identified their symptoms in an activity, and it was clear that regardless of their condition many shared the same problems. These were pain, tiredness, poor mobility and also psychological issues such as stress, anxiety, isolation and lack of confidence. One key feature was about empowerment, so we included exercises on assertiveness. We encouraged them to develop specific action plans about small specific changes they wanted to make and to carry them through.

Many of the participants suffered from mental health issues and said they felt frustrated, angry, isolated and depressed about their condition. So we built in activities about positivity which did seem to help. Saying something like "I am happy, I am valued, I can do it," in front of a mirror can work wonders for self-esteem. One young woman spoke about the frustration when her fibromyalgia flared up. She had to choose between washing her hair or taking her daughter to school, as she only had enough energy for one activity. This caused a feeling of guilt and other participants said they felt they were a burden. We introduced a range of activities to deal with confidence and self-compassion.

We asked people to complete a survey at the start and end of the course, and most reported an improved mood and confidence. This was very subjective and not very scientific, but we collected the views of 488 participants across Scotland:

- 60% reported an improvement in their ability to cope with pain.
- 80% said they learned about how access to and participation in appropriate exercise helps them manage their condition.
- 100% reported benefitting from meeting and sharing with others, and feeling more hopeful and positive.

Participants shared ideas about practical chores and activities they found relaxing. We provided some stimulus materials and encouraged them to write poems. Here are some of the examples from five of the group (all aged over 80) that they produced in just half an hour:

Wellbeing courses in Monifieth.

Our wee Sally was awfy glum,
So she joined our group to have some fun.
We chat and laugh and forget our ails
But she wished there were more males.

Lis and Gaye have made our day
By showing us how to lead the way.
Self-care we are learning fast.
Relying on others is a thing of the past.

This is definite not my forte,
So I'll go somewhere and just be naughty.
But where to go I haven't a clue,
So I'm passing this problem on to you.
Would tell you more, but I am fly,
And the other reason is my pen's run dry.

I once had a cat called Nellie
Who loved you to scratch her belly.
She purred so hard she frightened herself,
And ran up the curtains to the top shelf.

Mossy, damp, cool.
What do I see
as I look in the pool?

Ripples, mist, sunlight.
The peace I feel
watching water flow.
Dripping, rushing, bubbling,
Moving along the stream
leads me on.
Time that passes as I sit here
gives me the freedom to dream.

We are such a merry band
With sore legs and stiff hands.
We do not moan but have a laugh.
Of misery we've had enough.
The coffee's good and so's the location.
It's doon the road by the railway station.

I am an experienced trainer, but I am used to teaching academic subjects to university students. I quickly realised that I had to adapt my style to suit members of the general public with varying levels of education and literacy. Working with participants who were deaf was enlightening for me. I assumed that having words on the slides would help them. But I had not realised that English was not their first language, and many had a reading age of about eight years old. British Sign Language was their preferred mode of communication. Fortunately a signer was provided to translate everything and we all learned a few signs. At Christmas we sang and signed carols and it was incredibly moving.

We delivered a version of the course for Capability Scotland for adults with a range of physical and learning disabilities. The participants did not have medical problems so we shifted the focus to aspects of diet, exercise, creativity and

Wellbeing course, Deaf Hub, with signer.

communication and included lots of singing. We all enjoyed singing and doing the actions for "Simon Says", "Food Glorious Food", "The Hokey Cokey" and "If You're Happy and You Know it, Clap Your Hands". Some were initially quite reserved. I remember one young lady who would not meet my eyes or shake my hand on the first day. But three weeks later she brought in some photographs just to show me. I was so proud of having made that connection. Some of these participants were visually impaired so we included tactile activities with objects and gentle movement exercises. We called the course "Well! Well! Well!" and turned the action planning task into a wishing well.

The next adaptation of the wellbeing course was for university students who had a chronic condition, many of them with mental health issues. I ran several courses called "Wellbeing Regardless" under the auspices of disabil-

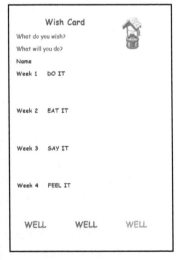

Exemplar wish card.

ity services. The aim was to help them enjoy university life to the full and to find strategies that worked for them in balancing their academic demands with their social life while dealing with their condition. Relaxation and stress management exercises really helped, as did the mutual peer support.

I always used the action plan approach, asking them to identify a specific goal to work towards. One young person who looked like a female announced that she wanted to grow a beard and explained she was transitioning to a male. I asked about the stages in the journey, and they explained about counselling and hormone injections. The other participants were really supportive and one male student with a sizeable beard talked about the practicalities of beard hygiene. It is difficult to know which pronouns to use in this paragraph, but there was no discomfort in the group discussion.

Once the pandemic hit and impacted on teaching methods I delivered the course by an online computer conferencing system. Some students were more comfortable in this anonymous environment. Some preferred to put their microphone on but not their camera. Some were happy speaking, others commented by typing messages via the chat box, and others only commented on an anonymous electronic flipchart. I included more activities on relaxation and mindfulness and added in a poem at the end of each session. The course was still val-

Well, Well, Well course,
Capability Scotland.

uable, but I felt it suffered by not having the face-to-face encounters to develop trust. Here are some of the comments from the participants:

- I really enjoyed this course! It's given me a lot of coping mechanisms on things I had struggled with.
- I feel less alone with my issues since I've been able to speak to others with similar problems. Good to know I'm not alone in my struggles and feelings.
- Thought provoking.
- Very useful hints and tips – food, exercise, and being more assertive.
- The wellbeing audit really spoke to me – it's ok to scale down the 'high aspects', so you can concentrate on your work-life balance.

The latest version of the course, still using Zoom, was aimed at any students. I called it "Give It Some Welly" to show it related to empowerment and wellbeing. The focus was on resilience, positive thinking and coping strategies. I covered managing time, dealing with stress, and living with change and uncertainty. I included mindful activities, encouraged them to share practical ideas, gave them thought-provoking poems and helped them identify specific action plans.

At the end I sent out a manual containing key ideas and hot links to useful websites. Here are some of the comments from the students:

- I cannot thank you enough for this. It is absolutely timely.
- Truly grateful.
- May your good deeds come back to you a million times.
- I have been struggling but I'll try to be more positive in future.
- Thank you for so many great ideas.

I try to maintain my own wellbeing by regular meditation, walking every day, a healthy lifestyle and a positive frame of mind. Sometimes it is easier than others, but I believe that gratitude and self-compassion are key elements.

Chapter Eleven

Creativity and Fun

I am not artistic or musical, but I do believe in lateral thinking and I have used a range of creative approaches to motivate students. I use quizzes, competitive debates and laughter yoga. I encourage students to use mind-maps to show links between topics. I teach and use participatory methods of evaluation using Post-It notes, postcards, card sorts and games. Sometimes the physicality of moving coloured pieces of card or drawing a concept can engage people more than a discussion.

I have a bag of unusual objects that I use to elicit reactions. People are very creative with their responses and they stimulate more ideas in others. Here are some typical comments:

Why is your object...	Because...
like a good lecturer?	the racing car depends on good teamwork for success.
like an effective student?	the cotton makes strong stitches and I make links between different subjects.

| useful for your wellbeing? | the shoeshine reminds me that taking care of my appearance boosts my morale. |
| helpful in managing your illness? | the calendar tells me to order my medication and to monitor my health. |

I also collect and create pictures and use them to stimulate discussion on various topics. I spread the pictures out and ask participant to choose an image that:

- describes your relationship with your students
- explains how your illness makes you feel
- explores the management system in your organisation.

On one occasion, one of the participants recognised the photograph of a group of yachts as it contained her own boat. She was no longer able to sail and was quite emotional when I said she could keep the picture. My collection of cards, like my bag of objects, became well known and colleagues would often borrow them for use in their own classes.

One Christmas I idly looked at all the cards displayed on my walls and noticed patterns. There were lots of robins and snowmen and Christmas

Some sample contents from my famous bag of objects.

trees; some had messages, some were religious. I devised a workshop activity to teach about the thematic analysis of evaluative comments which would be part of my module on evaluation methodology. I collected more Christmas cards from colleagues and used just the pictures, discarding the personal greetings. I put students into small groups and gave them 25 cards to sort into no more than five categories. Then I gave them 25 more cards to add and they often realised they had to change their categories. The real learning came during the debrief, when it became clear the challenges of this simulation could be applied to analysing qualitative comments from evaluation questionnaires:

- Does a dove go into the bird category or the religious category?
- If a card has a robin and a snowman, do you tear it in half, choose the largest image, or make a copy and put it in two categories?
- If you have a single card that does not fit any category do you ignore it?

This usually led to a lively debate relating to examples from their own experiences. One person thought about ignoring a comment about a broken lift until she realised it was from a student

My collection of cards and photos.

in a wheelchair and was very significant. This activity was popular, and colleagues again borrowed the cards to repeat my workshop. But I became concerned that it might seem to be culturally insensitive since it was linked to a Christian festival. There had never been any complaints, but I stopped using it.

I have always been happy to share my ideas and resources with my colleagues, and frequently lent out my piles of Christmas cards together with action handouts for analysing the clusters and relating this to the process of thematic analysis. I was surprised to see a new lecturer deliver "my" workshop for his teaching observation for the PGCAPHE. He had been given the material by another colleague, and he had not realised it originated with me. I turned this into a learning conversation about intellectual property and professional ethics.

I used poetry in a workshop about assessment. I asked everyone to write a poem and then to swap with a partner and give each other feedback. I asked for a cinquain, and gave them the criteria for the task along with a couple of examples I had written.

WRITE A CINQUAIN
Criteria:
Five lines
The number of syllables in each line is
2, 4, 6, 8, 2.
Last line has impact.
Use normal English grammar and spelling.
Suggested topics: an animal, an emotion.
You may give your poem a title if you wish.

BURIED

Rain, moss
And grey lichen
Hide the names on gravestones.
So who remembers the people?
No-one!

Purring,
Scratching, clawing,
Curious, miaowing,
Independent, affectionate.
Feline.

When we debriefed the exercise, most people had given feedback about the aesthetic aspects of the poem, even though they were not part of the criteria. This led to a rich discussion about objective criteria (e.g. number of syllables, grammar, spelling, task completion) and more subjective criteria (e.g. humour, originality of ideas, use of language). The quality of the poems they wrote was often very high.

I used practical creative exercises in several wellbeing courses. I used pictures from magazines to stimulate poetry writing. I encouraged people to do abstract paintings, and supported a group to design a collage about Dundee. In all cases the participants focused on the task in hand and were keen to share ideas and provide mutual support.

There are many models of curriculum design, and one popular activity with new lecturers was to ask them for theirs. I started with a "brainstorm". I still use that term, even though it was outlawed for a while. Some politically correct person said that using an activity which included the word "storm" might be distressing to some students, so it was replaced with the term "thought shower". This was later dropped when some male students said it made them think about girls in the shower! Lecturers brainstormed all the elements they needed to consider when planning a curriculum. Then they designed a model. Some created beautiful colourful representations. One architecture lecturer made a 3D paper model. The explanations for the designs were fascinating. They took various formats such as a matrix, tree, spider's web, star or spiral. There were different central starting points such as the subject matter, future employers, the student or the lecturer. I personally prefer a more student-centred view but I know of several programmes where the choice of modules was dictated by the interests and knowledge of the tutors without any academic rationale or consideration of student needs.

I often use my "Rose or Daisy" activity at the start of a workshop. It helps people identify their own personal qualities and consider if others perceive them in the same way. I ask each person to choose between two items and write one of them on a piece of paper. Are you more like a rose (elegant but with thorns) or a daisy (commonplace but resilient)? Then I ask people to find someone with a similar list and to discuss their interpretation of the qualities. I have listed some typical responses below but of course there are no correct answers, although it is a good stimulus to get people thinking and sharing insights.

ROSE	elegant, thorny	OR	commonplace, resilient	DAISY
CAT	independent, aloof	OR	loyal, syco-phantic	DOG
SUN	warm, bright	OR	cold, romantic	MOON
RIVER	purposeful, energetic	OR	reflective, stagnant	LAKE
OAK	reliable, re-sponsive	OR	straight, con-stant	PINE

I have always been a keen evening class student and have attended courses on pottery, painting, art appreciation, English literature, gardening, drama, creative writing, local history and physical

The Nethergate Writers at Waterstones Dundee

exercise. I have also taken a range of online courses on aspects of education, wellbeing, creative writing, mindfulness, history and health.

I joined a creative writing class for several years. We critiqued each other's work and produced a themed project or book every year. We were called the Nethergate Writers. One time we visited the university's archive collection and used the artefacts to stimulate short stories. Another time we had a tour of the Queen's Hotel and all wrote stories based there. The photo above shows the launch of our collection on ancestry, called *Roots*, in the Waterstones bookshop in Dundee.

One of the exercises in the class was to create a poem quickly in response to a stimulus, and I began doing this when I visited tourist attractions. Here are some of the things I wrote, though I think I would call them doggerel rather than poetry.

Strachur Smiddy

The heat from the forge
is a blast from the past,
Which proves that old skills
Really do last.

Strachur Churchyard

The rusty park bench is my pew;
My church: the open air.
May all good wishes go with you
As God is everywhere.

Lichen-covered tombstones
Marking every grave
Telling family stories,
Some good, some sad, some brave.

A Drowned Martyr

(*Margaret Wilson aged 18 was executed for her faith on
11 May 1685. She was tied to a stake in Wigtown Bay
and drowned by the incoming tide.*)

She was tied to the martyr's stake
While gulls pecked in the mud.
She was punished for Jesus' sake
They flew before the flood.

She shivered as her arms were bare.
The waves lapped at her dress.
The wind blew gently through her hair,
Immune to her distress.

The water swirled around her waist.
Her legs were numb with cold.
Her fear was all that she could taste.
She never would grow old.

A future life she never had,
So she thought of her past.
She felt so angry, scared and sad.
Her ordeal would not last.

Though just eighteen her faith was sure.
She prayed with certainty.
Her body and her soul are pure
For all eternity.

Auchindrain

(*an open-air museum of ancient cottages*)

We wandered through old Auchindrain
Over rough and rugged terrain.
The centuries tumble,
The cottages crumble
Back to nature again.

Taynish

(a nature reserve in Argyll)

Thirty different wild flowers.
Gently passing happy hours.
Grief abating,
Joy awaiting
A peaceful future.

The North Yorks Moors Steam Railway

Clickety clack.
Clickety clack.

The line is steep.
Scatter the sheep
Over the track
On the way back.

Billowing steam,
Bubbling stream,
Heath and thistle.
Sound the whistle.

Clickety clack.
Clickety clack.

My Dad had been a pilot in World War II and he had been sent to Canada, the USA and South Africa as well as many camps in Britain. After his death I found 400 letters he had sent to my Mum between 1940 and 1946. He talked about his love for her, the exhilaration of learning to fly, and the sadness on the death of his colleagues. He discussed literature and philosophy, and wrote a lot about food – wonderful banquets in private homes in South Africa and starvation rations on troopships. He never considered that they might not win the war. I turned the letters into a book, adding explanatory comments and details about their life before and after the war. Montrose Air Museum digitised his old photos, which added an extra dimension of authenticity to the book. When Extremis published *Waiting in the Wings* I revelled in the connection to my parents.

Some of my most memorable and inspirational experiences have been in large lectures. The University of Dundee has run public lectures for over eighty years. The audience is in the hundreds and there is no interaction, yet the power of good speakers is amazing. With a carefully crafted delivery of knowledge and the passion of personal experience, such speakers are entertainers as well as teachers. Three spring to mind, although they were some years ago. The first is Jung Chang the author of *Wild Swans* who spoke movingly about living in China. Joe Morrow, Lord Lyon King of Arms, talked about the history of the crests enlightened by stories of some of the more unusual applicants such as sports clubs and schools. Professor Dame Sue Black talked about her work as a forensic anthropologist in solving murders and investigating war crimes. She spoke about the need for cadavers as learning resources for medical students and inspired me to sign the forms and donate my own body to the university.

Afterword

The pandemic forced us to adopt new ways of teaching and learning. It was very challenging and exhausting for my colleagues and their students and I was, in some ways, glad that I was retired. I shared my thoughts about the future of higher education, but I think they really just represent my own philosophy, regardless of Covid restrictions.

The New Normal for Learning and Teaching

We should take this opportunity to make our teaching more effective and to create learners who become self-evaluating professionals. We need learners who are able to take responsibility for their own learning, so we should increase student autonomy and metacognition. Here are some practical approaches:

Increase learning effectiveness
Provide activities to encourage students to:
- explore how they learn best.
- accept that different types of learning work best in different situations.

- identify their own support map.

See the learning in context
Make sure the students get the full benefit from a module by getting them to:
- turn the learning outcomes and assessment criteria in the module specification into their own language.
- identify explicit links between modules.
- discuss how the module might help with their future career.
- realise the specific and generic (transferable) learning.
- use an evolving list of questions in which they make a list of questions at the start, tick them off as they learn the answers, and add more questions as they become apparent.

Learn as you go
- Build on the idea of "assessment is for learning" by having formative activities throughout the module including self, peer and group assessments.
- Create small learning teams that work together on tasks, with each student taking a turn at leading and reporting.
- Use flipped learning by putting resources on the VLE followed by individual or group activities.

Gaye Manwaring
14.5.20

Over the years I have watched educational developments gradually giving more autonomy to students. The pandemic has encouraged the growth of blended and flexible learning approaches:

Individualised Learning	Students study learning materials at their own pace.
Distance Learning	Students study learning materials at their own pace and place.
Open Learning	Students study learning materials (often online) at their own pace and place.
Blended Learning	Mix of face-to-face and online learning.
Flipped Learning	Online learning followed by face-to-face learning
HyFlex Learning	Student chooses face-to-face, online synchronous and online asynchronous classes.

Flipped and HyFlex learning can require heavy workload from staff, and clear induction is needed so students take responsibility. This empowerment builds confidence as well as learning. It can begin the fight against injustice.

Many universities identify the attributes they expect all graduates to display. I have devised my own list of key attributes for university lecturers, and they are personal characteristics linked to my philosophy of teaching and learning.

- Facilitation and promotion of learning
- Social interaction and support
- Reflection

- Resilience
- Creativity and curiosity
- Compassion and empathy
- Professional and ethical behaviour

These are appropriate qualities for students too. Lecturers can strive to develop them in themselves and in their students. They are actually human attributes, regardless of a career.

I was once asked what I thought was the single most important quality for a lecturer. My reply was "Respect". This is a broad concept including the championing of differences, the support of individuals as well as the development of self-confidence. I can turn it into an acrostic.

R	Reflection
E	Empathy
S	Support
P	Professionalism
E	Empowerment
C	Creativity
T	Truth

This is the end of this book.

Curriculum Vitae

Gaye Manwaring MBE BSc PhD FRSA FHEA

Higher Education

1963-66	BSc (Honours) Zoology, University of Exeter
1966-67	PG Diploma in Animal Genetics, University of Edinburgh
1967-73	PhD in Biochemical Genetics, University of Edinburgh
1975-76	Teaching Qualification (Secondary, Zoology), Dundee College of Education
1986	Member of the Order of the British Empire
1992	Fellow of the Royal Society of Arts
2000	Fellow of the Institute for Teaching and Learning in Higher Education
2011	Coaching Skills Certificate, Napier University
2012	Advanced Facilitation and Presentation Skills, Befriending Network, SQA

Employment

1969-75	Research Fellow, Inter-university Biology Teaching Project, Glasgow University Part time Lecturer, Extra-mural Department
1975-87	Senior Lecturer, Dundee College of

Education, Course Director for CNAA Post-graduate Diploma in Educational Technology

1987-01	Principal Lecturer, Coordinator of Tertiary Education, Northern College of Education
2000-05	Programme Leader, Teaching Qualification in Further Education
2001-20	Senior Lecturer, University of Dundee Module Leader: PGCAPHE, BAPD, BACP, MSc, MEd

Consultancy Work

1974	Invited speaker, Eighth International conference on Educational Technology, Poznan, Poland
1974	Study Tour of USA and Canada
1976-89	Honorary Lecturer, Centre for Medical Education, University of Dundee
1978,79	Visiting lecturer, Universiti Sains Malaysia, Penang (plus workshops in Kuala Lumpar and Bangkok)
1979	Visiting fellow, Murdoch University, Perth, Australia (plus workshops in Canberra and Sydney)
1987-98	Director, Medical Open Learning Service (externally funded)
1989-95	Project Leader SOED Staff Development and Appraisal Training (externally funded)
2008	Invited to run workshops in University of Zagreb, Croatia

Publications

Journal articles and chapters: 35
Educational Packages (various media; online) : 23
Learning units and modules (print; audiovisual; online):
numerous

Acknowledgements

I am so grateful to all my colleagues and students who have contributed to my experiences over so many years. Many friends and colleagues encouraged me to write this book, especially Cathie, Elizabeth, Eddie, Helen, Joyce, Kate, Lorraine, Pete and Richard. Elizabeth retrieved some documents and photographs from the attic. I am particularly thankful to Jill Shimi, student, colleague, peer mentor and friend, for many editorial comments on early drafts. My thanks too to Ian Ball for many collaborative events as well as writing the Foreword. My husband, Andy Wilson, as always has helped and motivated me. Julie and Tom Christie from Extremis Publishing not only published the book, but advised on many aspects and shot some of the photographs.

Thank you all.

About the Author

Dr Gaye Manwaring recently retired from the University of Dundee after a long career in higher education. She lives in Dundee with her husband and they enjoy travelling Scotland in their motorhome. She is involved in voluntary work linked to resilience and wellbeing. Her other interests include reading, writing, theatre, nature, cats and social history.

Waiting in the Wings

Letters of a Pilot in World War II

By Gaye Manwaring

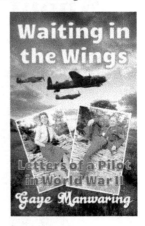

The Second World War left no corner of Europe unaffected, and was to touch lives in every country. Young British librarian Len Manwaring was no exception; answering his country's call to arms, he would soon discover a life turned upside down when he enlisted in the Royal Air Force and saw a tour of duty which involved time serving in North America and South Africa as well as closer to home in a United Kingdom that was fighting the constant threat of invasion. Yet just as difficult for Len was the prospect of leaving behind Joan, the girl he loved, with whom he would correspond throughout the entirety of the war.

Now, in this special anthology of letters, airgraphs and other authentic materials from the time, Gaye Manwaring presents the remarkable story of her parents' extraordinary romance, set against the backdrop of an era-defining global conflict. Illustrated with many photographs from the 1940s, Waiting in the Wings is the story of how true love can endure in the most challenging of circumstances - even a war which saw Len and Joan separated not just by their duties in the armed services, but by the distance which lay between whole continents.

Presented with social and personal commentary from the author throughout, Waiting in the Wings is a unique account of a love affair that stood the trials of war and the test of time; a timely reminder that light can shine in even the darkest days.

For details of new and forthcoming books
from Extremis Publishing, including our
podcasts, please visit our official website at:

www.extremispublishing.com

or follow us on social media at:

www.facebook.com/extremispublishing

www.linkedin.com/company/extremis-publishing-ltd-/